DARTMOUTH

Seventy-five years in pictures

Frontispiece
The Front of the College, Spring 1972.
(Charles Risk.)

DARTMOUTH

Seventy-five years in pictures

E L DAVIES & E J GROVE

Gieves & Hawkes

Published in Great Britain in 1980 by
Gieves & Hawkes Limited, 22, The Hard, Portsmouth, Hampshire

ISBN 0–85997–462–6

Photoset, printed and bound in Great Britain by
Redwood Burn Limited, Trowbridge & Esher.

Contents

Acknowledgments

Many people have helped us to write this book, by giving us of their time, knowledge or possessions, and we are grateful to them all. Some we cannot thank at all, and many we cannot thank enough. We hope they will take no offence if we merely list their names here, and that any we may have omitted will accept our general thanks. Of our colleagues at the College, we would like especially to mention Kenrick Armitstead, Robert Avery, Chris Earle, Richard Kennel, Robin Macpherson, Michael Scott-Scott, Robin Tonks, and John Wood. The photographic department has laboured hard, often over doubtful negatives, and always under pressure of time: Charles Risk is deserving of the greatest thanks for his efforts.

We would also like to mention many people from outside the College: former members of staff, former students and friends who have helped us. Notable among these have been the Lord Strathclyde of Barskimming, the Lady Serpell, John Barlee, Captain N Dalrymple-Hamilton, Miss C Dalrymple-Hamilton, the Rt Rev G K Giggal, A Stirling Gordon, Lt-Cdr J Haddock, Commander W A E Hall, David Hannaford, Mrs J Hicks, Brigadier W Hine-Haycock, Lt-Cdr A Hogg, Mrs D Holwill, the late Mrs B Horne, Rev R H Horne (Mrs Elmes), Mrs J Howard, R Hunter, Commander H L Jenkins, Mrs E R Joslyn, Mrs A G Joyce, Mrs G P van de Kasteele and Miss van de Kasteele, Lt-Cdr C J J Kemp, Canon M Kennedy, Lt-Cdr J B Lamb, R B P Land, Lt-Cdr E S W Maclure, H E May, Captain C H H Owen, Mrs A K Pearce, Captain W Peek, G Price, Lt-Cdr G Read, Commander J C Richards, Captain J K Robertson, John F Scott, Captain J C K Slater, Lt-Cdr R Vaughan-Cox, Mrs K Willett, Mrs M Wilson.

These kind people have all helped, as have the staffs of the National Maritime Museum, Imperial War Museum and Public Record Office. But we have made our own mistakes, though we hope very few have survived to be printed.

Finally we would like to dedicate this book, as a thank-you, to Anthea and Elizabeth, who have put up with much, including loss of dining rooms and variety in topics of conversation, over the last few months.

Evan Davies,
Eric Grove.

Foreword

The Britannia Royal Naval College Dartmouth has a special place in our affairs. It is here that virtually all officers start their careers which will lead some through command at sea to the Admiralty Board.

There have been many changes since Dartmouth was first commissioned in 1905. Formerly it trained Cadets who joined as 13-year old schoolboys (I was one) with half their general education still before them. Now it is concerned with midshipmen and sub lieutenants, doctors, dentists and chaplains, WRNS and QARNNS, whose ages range from the late teens to the early thirties. About one sixth are from friendly countries overseas. Dartmouth today is neither a public school nor a university; it is a naval college.

DPR (N)

The College reflects the progress of the Navy as a whole since the turn of the century. Our ships and weapons, our conduct of operations and tactics, our methods and skills have changed radically; our values, professionalism and purpose remain unswervingly the same. Dartmouth concentrates on Leadership.

The Royal Navy enters the 80s confident that the qualities and standards instilled at Dartmouth will match the many challenges into the next century as effectively as it has for the past 75 years. This is a great task and a great trust.

Henry Leach

Admiral Sir Henry Leach, GCB, ADC
Chief of the Naval Staff and
First Sea Lord.

Introduction

A College is Built – 1863–1905

The training of new entry officers first came to Dartmouth almost forty-two years before the opening of the present College. About 10 a.m. on September 30th 1863 the training ship HMS *Britannia* was towed to her mooring in the river Dart by Mill Creek. Exposure, first to the fleshpots of Portsmouth and then to the strong winds of Portland, had driven the three-decker and her 230 cadets to a safer and more suitable home with its easy access to the shore and nearby land for playing fields. The two-decker *Hindostan* arrived the next year and was joined to *Britannia* to provide more accommodation. The latter was still hardly big enough, however, and, with question marks raised over her healthiness, she was replaced in 1869 by the three-decker *Prince of Wales*, which had been launched in 1860 but had never been to sea. She was now completed as a training hulk, and renamed as the fifth HMS *Britannia*.

Despite this improvement, the problems created by crowding two to three hundred boys into two static wooden ships still caused concern and in 1874 a Committee was appointed chaired by Rear Admiral E B Rice to look into both the health and general training of cadets. In its report of 1875 it recommended that a College building should be constructed on shore and in July of the following year another Committee, on the 'Acquisition of a site for a Naval Cadets' College', met under the chairmanship of Admiral G G Wellesley. It considered thirty-two sites, not only at Dartmouth and Kingswear but on the Isle of Wight and Southampton Water, at Gosport, Hayling Island, Portsmouth, Weymouth, Devonport, Milford Haven and even Westward Ho!

Advertisements were placed in the newspapers and both local pride and hopes for financial gain were enlisted to obtain and evaluate proposals. The dispute became both public and rather acrimonious and the front-runners emerged as Wootton in the Isle of Wight and 'Mount Boon' (sic) at Dartmouth. In the end the Wellesley Committee came down heavily in favour of the latter, the location of the existing Britannia playing fields. It was a site 'admirable . . . in all respects, possessing every requisite, the only drawback being the large amount of rainfall and a certain amount of inconvenience in the movements of a training vessel without the use of steam'.

Nothing happened. The exact reasons are unclear but expense was probably the main culprit. In the 'Dark Ages of the Victorian Navy' economy was the watchword and the decision of the Prince of Wales to send his sons to the existing *Britannia* seemed a vote of confidence in the old ship. Criticism continued and yet another Committee, in 1885, raised local hackles by recommending the removal of training to the Solent. This proposal was forgotten when further public grumbles about Britannia's 'gaol-like' atmosphere and discipline problems resurrected the College idea in the mid 1890s. Naval expenditure had regained popularity and the Admiralty was committing itself to ambitious programmes funded by an almost profligate series of financial loans. 'Preliminary discussion' of the 'Britannia Establishment, Sick Quarters etc' took place at Board of Admiralty level on 15th November 1895 along with proposals to revise the existing training scheme. When presenting the Naval Estimates in March 1896, Mr George Goschen, the First Lord, announced that the decision to build a College at Dartmouth had been taken and that the scheme of training offered, first in the ship and then in the new shore establishment, would be altered to four shorter terms of four months each. Cadets would enter at between fourteen-and-a-half and fifteen-and-a-half, a year older than previously.

The instruction to begin negotiations to buy the land for the new College had in fact been given in February and Treasury clearance for the expenditure was requested. The chosen site at Mount Boone was already used for the *Britannia*'s playing fields and the kennels for the Beagle pack, but it would now have to be purchased outright. The Raleigh Estate, to which it belonged, was still in Chancery, however, and the negotiations soon became complex and difficult. By October they had effectively broken down and the Admiralty began to consider compulsory purchase for £25,000. It hoped that the legislation under which the College was to be funded, the Naval Works Loan Act of 1895, gave it the required powers but legal advice was to the contrary and the Defence Act of 1842 had to be resorted to instead. By December the land for purchase had been marked out but acquisition was still held up due to disputes over Dartmouth's status as a 'fortress' or 'garrison' town. Judgement was not finally given in favour of the Admiralty until 13th November 1897 and the owners' representatives, seeing the futility of further resistance, became more cooperative in order to secure the best possible price. The final settlement seems to have been made at the end of June 1898.

Aston Webb was chosen as architect and work began on the terraces that year; not until later were tenders requested for the construction of the buildings themselves. On 18th April 1900 the Admiralty accepted the submission from Higgs and Hill who estimated they could build the College in three and a half years at a cost of £220,600.

Work proceeded throughout 1901, a year which saw a particularly serious influenza epidemic in the ships with the death of two cadets. This may have led to the work on the new sick quarters being speeded up for they soon began to take shape ahead of the rest of the College. By March 1902 the main building had also begun to rise and on the 7th of that month King Edward VII laid the foundation stone. The new hospital took its first patient at the beginning of the autumn term.

Shortly afterwards, on Christmas Day, 1902, was published the 'Selborne Memorandum' on officer entry and training. All new officers of the Executive and Engineer branches of the Royal Navy, and of the Royal Marines, were to enter between the ages of 12 and 13 and be trained on exactly the same system until passing for the rank of Sub Lieutenant. The stress was on the importance of study for the creation of a competent officer for the new technological era.

The real power behind the new scheme was not the First Lord but Admiral Sir John Fisher, the Second Sea Lord. The latter's dynamism put the proposals into effect as soon as possible. 'Britannia Royal Naval College' was still far from ready and was, in any case, unsuitable for the new scheme without modification. Before the end of 1902, therefore, plans had been made for a new College in the grounds of Queen Victoria's house at Osborne on the Isle of Wight and construction began in March 1903. Within six months the new institution was opened by the King and its first term joined in September. They and their successors were to spend six terms (two years), at Osborne, before passing on for a similar period to Dartmouth. In order to provide accommodation for the two extra terms a new block containing a single large gunroom was begun on the east side of the existing works at Dartmouth.

As the revised College took shape during 1904 it was decided not to open it until September of the next year when the first 'new scheme' term would be ready to move from Osborne. The 'old scheme' had had to be kept going in order to keep a steady flow of officers into the service and when the College opened, there would still be two terms in the ships along with a new term joining. Captain Cross of *Britannia* assumed they, and his staff, would just transfer

The College nearing completion. Scaffolding can be seen along parts of the front, there is no clock, there are some huts along the terraces, and Mount Boone Farm is still being demolished. (*Photo College Archive*).

up the hill to the College that had, after all, been built for them. He was soon disabused. The architects of the 'new scheme' wanted the College to maintain as few of the old *Britannia*'s traditions as possible. Its teaching, which emphasised cramming for examinations, was anathema to educational progressives such as Professor J A Ewing, who had been appointed Director of Naval Education from Cambridge in 1903, and Cyril Ashford, first headmaster of Osborne and headmaster designate of Dartmouth. They wished the new College to emphasise the responsibility of the pupil to educate himself. They were joined by Rosslyn Wemyss, Captain of Osborne, in stressing the need for a 'fresh start'. As Wemyss and Ewing put it in the summer of 1904 'the development of the College should proceed with the least possible influence on the part of the old system of training'. Ewing was even stronger in a slightly later paper; 'I am very anxious to see that Dartmouth College develops on entirely new lines without *Britannia* interference or even influence'. Opening with three *Britannia* terms to only one moved up from Osborne would mean that the scene would be dominated by the older boys prejudiced against the new order.

Captain Cross was totally outgunned in this bureaucratic engagement and, supported by Selborne, the Admiralty concocted a radical plan to deal with the problem. When the new College opened the fourth 'old scheme' term would depart to the cruiser HMS *Isis* in the normal way. The other two terms would also be loaded into cruisers to be taken to a foreign port to complete the work they would have done in *Britannia* or the new College. HMS *Eclipse* would take the third term and HMS *Highflyer* the second. Various sites were evaluated, all in tropical climes so that money could be saved on heating. Gibraltar, Malta, Alexandria, Los Palmas and the West Indies were all considered and the choice eventually fell on Bermuda.

So the *Britannia* contribution to the new College was kept to a minimum and Wemyss, who left Osborne in the Spring of 1905, was given the supervision of both Colleges to make sure the Admiralty's intentions were carried out. Cross left *Britannia* at the end of the Spring and was replaced by Captain Goodenough who would be directly responsible for the changeover. Commander Brand and nine other officers would also be from the *Britannia* but almost half of the initial naval staff would be new. Although the penultimate 'old scheme' term would arrive at the same time as the ex-Osborne cadets, it was the former who would be outnumbered by the latter, rather than vice versa. All the cadets would be taught by a new teaching staff in an institution firmly dedicated to the new scheme. The *Britannia* name might remain for a short time and, indeed, rather contrary to Ewing's wishes, the administration of the new College would owe a great deal to that of the old ships. Nevertheless, a remarkable amount had been done to ensure that September 1905 would indeed mark that 'clean break' with the past that Ewing and Ashford desired so much.

A School for Naval Officers – 1905–1955

Britannia Royal Naval College opened at last on September 14th 1905. The new building, 'a cross between a workhouse and a stable' as one critic had denounced it, stood out rather harshly in red and white on Mount Boone. It symbolised the new approach to naval education which Fisher and his lieutenants were imposing on a doubting service. The College contained only two terms, the sixty-three new scheme 'St Vincents' from Osborne and the forty-two 'Hawkes', who, as old-schemers, were new entries. The 'term' system kept the two groups almost entirely apart. Although the 'Hawkes' were older there was no doubt who were regarded as the most important.

In the summer of 1907 the College finally began to operate as intended with six new scheme terms, St Vincent, Drake, Blake, Hawke, Greynville and Rodney, the last two sharing 'C' Block. Each term was divided into 'watches' each of which was, in turn, subdivided into classes. 'Port A' was the most advanced class, 'Starboard B' the least. The College now contained 359 cadets although the maximum capacity was rated at over 400. Even so, there was too much pressure on the teaching accommodation of the original design. This situation was improved a little by the opening in 1907 of a new one-storey block with five additional studies and a reference library (the present 'E' Block). Naturally the staff also grew and at the beginning of 1908, when the *Britannia* was dropped even from the College title, Captain D W Napier of HMS *Espiegle*, Royal Naval College, Dartmouth, was commanding a naval staff that had increased from 20 to 29. Ashford now controlled twenty-six masters and four naval instructors.

The education offered by Ashford and his masters seems to have been notable both for its quality and novelty. The mathematics and science, supplemented by considerable practical engineering instruction, added together to create a grounding in applied science unique in contemporary secondary education. It even produced one winner of the Nobel Prize for Physics, Professor Lord Blackett who entered Dartmouth as a 'Hawke' in 1912. The humanities were not forgotten, however. Indeed the attempt to develop the intellects of the boys through the medium of Modern Languages, History and English rather than the Classics was as novel as the technological emphasis of the Royal Naval College Course. It is, perhaps, not too much to say that, in the context of its time, the early Dartmouth was one of the most progressive schools in the land.

As the Royal Navy expanded, the terms tended to increase in size, with seventy cadets in each becoming the norm. Among them was the Prince of Wales who joined as an 'Exmouth' in 1909, this name having replaced 'Rodney'. Prince Albert, later King George VI, arrived as a 'Greynville' in 1911.

The demand for officers was still increasing and, in 1913, the 'Special Entry' was begun for boys who had completed their education at public school. They would be trained separately from the cadets of the Selborne Scheme. It was also planned to increase the entries at the Royal Naval Colleges to an average of 110 per term. This was almost double the original numbers so extra accommodation would be required at both Colleges. A new block was therefore projected at Dartmouth to house three new large gunrooms, an extra dining hall and dormitories for the junior terms. Its construction allowed much needed extra laboratories, class rooms and a masters' common room to be added also. Construction began in the Summer of 1914 to the designs of Aston Webb's offices in 19 Queen Anne's Gate. It appears that, by this time, Webb no longer controlled the work that went on there. Certainly the inspiration of the original buildings was lacking in the new block which, much to the original architect's regret, ruined the roof line of the old College when seen from afar.

The First World War rudely interrupted life at Dartmouth. The Admiralty wished to utilise its cadets to provide midshipmen for the older ships of the reserve fleet and the boys took part in the test mobilisation of July 1914. They had been back in college for less than a week when Captain Stanley received the order to stand by to mobilise in earnest. Within seven hours the cadets and ship's company reservists were on their way to their war stations by train.

It was rumoured that the College building would be used as a naval hospital but a term of seventy-nine cadets joined from Osborne in September. The staff had been transformed. Stanley and almost all the other officers had gone to active service and been replaced by officers from the retired list. Rear Admiral P W Napier was commanding officer and the deputy headmaster, Arkwright and ten other masters had been lent to Osborne where three acted for a time as term officers as well as teachers. McMullen, the Head of Science, and three others had gone to sea as RNVR officers along with a mobilised retired list RN officer, and two others were serving with the Royal Engineers. M. Charbonnier of Modern Languages was serving in the French Army and two other modern linguists were at the Admiralty assisting Ewing with his secret intelligence work in 'Room 40'. Only Ashford, half a dozen masters and a naval instructor remained.

The College began to fill up again at the beginning of 1915 when two terms moved up from Osborne simultaneously along with most of the borrowed masters, and there were four terms back in residence by the start of the Summer term. In 1915–16 the time spent at Dartmouth by cadets fluctuated between three and five terms but the 'Exmouths' who entered in 1917 only spent a mere two terms at the College. Along with the two senior terms they were sent to sea in the summer of 1917. The Admiralty were considering Osborne's future and one of the options being explored was its abolition and the halving of the cadets' course. Moving three terms out of Dartmouth meant that the process could be begun and the same number of terms duly arrived from Osborne in September, along with four masters. The scheme was soon shelved, however, and the junior of these prematurely promoted terms spent an unprecedented eight terms at Dartmouth as did the following two entries.

The fluctuations in course length must have put a great strain on the academic staff and prevented them achieving even satisfactory results. The supervision of the superannuated naval officers also seems to have left something to be desired. Nevertheless, the College did not become overcrowded, even though the first of the larger terms arrived in 1916, long before the completion of the new buildings. The studies connecting the old buildings with the new were completed in May 1917 but the new block did not house its first cadets until the beginning of the next year. The opening of the new common room allowed the Headmaster to use the old one as a larger office.

The end of the war and the consequent contraction of the Royal Navy soon created considerable problems. Instead of recruiting reservists from civilian life as it would in the Second World War, the Admiralty had increased the numbers of regular officers and there were now far too many. The new terms arriving at Osborne were halved in size from the summer of 1919 but more drastic pruning was required. The blow fell on 30th March 1920. Captain Leatham announced to the cadets assembled on the quarterdeck that although the present senior term would pass out as it stood, the other four large terms, and the three similar-sized terms at Osborne, would have to be cut by 40%.

The departures seem to have been voluntary and not as great as originally intended. Nevertheless the new small entries meant that Dartmouth's enlarged accommodation could now include Osborne's cadets as well as the older boys. The junior college's reputation for disease had for some time rivalled that of the old 'Britannia' and the contemporary financial climate ruled out new properly built accommodation. Therefore the Admiralty decided to close RNC Osborne and in May 1920 two terms moved up to Dartmouth instead of one. In January 1921 two more arrived and in May the four remaining Osborne terms moved up along with the first new entries to join Dartmouth since the end of the old scheme. Captain Marten of Osborne had already replaced Leatham who had been promoted Rear Admiral. The last cadets left Osborne on 5th April and the junior college officially closed on 20th May.

Dartmouth settled down once more but now with eleven terms of over 500 cadets instead of six of 400. Engineering was reduced in importance and treated less practically as, with the Special Entry providing suitable candidates for the other branches, Dartmouth cadets were now intended to be Executive officers only. The new names chosen for the extra terms were Anson, Benbow, Hood, Rodney and Duncan. The large 'D' block gunrooms were divided by partitions and the terms began their progression around the College from the west end of that building. Junior terms messed in 'D' block mess-room, seniors in the main building. The teaching staff was swelled by ex-Osborne masters to 55 and the naval staff, also including ex-Osborne members, now totalled 39.

The 1920s were in some ways a 'Golden Age' in Dartmouth's history. Changes were few and after the traumas of the 'Geddes Axe' things seemed secure. Routine rather than innovation became the order of the day. As HM Inspector of Schools reported in 1926 in an otherwise complimentary report 'the staff was tending to become a smooth-running, efficient machine rather than a body of pioneers developing new ideas and a new system'. There does, however, seem to have been a little tension around this time between the Headmaster and the Captain, over the control of engineering instruction. It was a pity that this slight cloud marred Ashford's final years at Dartmouth for at the end of the summer term 1927 Dartmouth's first headmaster retired. A knighthood was a fitting reward for his magnificent services to naval education.

The new academic head was E W E Kempson who had originally worked as an engineer, and had taught at the College before the war as both a Naval Instructor and a civilian master. In 1911 he had gone to Rugby to head the science department and, after the war, in which he had served in the Royal Engineers and won the MC, he had become an Inspector of Schools. In their 1926 report the Inspectors had commented on the care given to the weaker pupils, but rather at the expense of the brighter cadets. Accordingly Kempson soon announced that 'Alpha' classes would be chosen in the three senior terms, members of which would concentrate on three main subjects at the expense of a fourth. These cadets were also given a slightly relaxed routine and expected to work more on their own.

As the economic horizon began to darken in 1929, the College began to come under attack in Parliament and the Press. As the number of cadets dropped faster than the numbers of staff employed in the College, concern and criticism mounted over the apparently lavish ratio of staff to pupils. In 1932 there were indeed 412 officers, masters, ship's company and civilian workers to only 408 cadets. It was suggested that Dartmouth might take pupils not intended for a service career but this proved unnecessary. Favourable reports from the schools inspectorate, the support of the Admiralty and cuts in staff all helped stave off closure. All terms except the first were grouped into pairs and by 1934, when the number of cadets was reduced to 368, there were only twenty officers and thirty-six masters (including two Naval Instructors). Total college staff had been cut to 308.

One important problem at this time was that parents, worried about the long term prospects of the naval profession, were preferring the flexibility of the Special Entry rather than committing their sons to Dartmouth at 13. By 1936 the numbers at the College had risen to 415 but only at some cost. As Kempson reported that year to the Admiralty, of the 45 places available for a recent term only 26 had passed for entrance but seventeen 'failures' had been allowed in to boost numbers, and even then the term had not been filled. This was in turn causing doubts to be expressed about RNC cadets when compared with the quality of the Special Entry. It was recognised by some that there were indeed, features of College life that were becoming unattractive.

These defects seem to have become clear to Admiral Sir Martin Dunbar-Nasmyth, Captain of the College 1926–29. When he was Second Sea Lord in 1936 he was the force behind the decision taken that year to introduce a house system. The new Captain, F H G Dalrymple-Hamilton arrived in January 1937 to supervise the change-over and he found Kempson to be an enthusiastic supporter of the idea. The two seem to have got on very well together. After a meeting with term officers the original proposal of seven houses was reduced to five and, in March, the Captain, with Lt Cdr Sladen, the 'Duncan' term officer, left on a 'whistle-stop' tour of public schools to see houses in action. After further discussion the new system was duly introduced at the beginning of the summer term. The houses were called St Vincent, Exmouth, Hawke, Blake and Grenville (new spelling), the first three to be accommodated in 'D' block, the last two in the front buildings ('A' and 'B' blocks respectively). 'C' block with its large gunroom was to be a junior 'Drake' house for the first two terms.

The process which has seen the emphasis at Dartmouth swing from academic study to professional training began in 1939. The deteriorating international situation had led to the Special Entries' training cruiser *Frobisher* being refitted for active service. In May, therefore, the eighteen-year-olds who should have gone to sea in her were sent instead to Dartmouth's ship's company barracks block.

Far from the exodus of 1914 the outbreak of war in 1939 saw the College dramatically increase in size. Another group of Special Entry cadets arrived and were housed in 'C' block owing to the barracks being still occupied by the 'Frobishers' and the RNC passing-out term who would also normally have been at sea. Extra huts had to be constructed to provide sufficient accommodation. The Drakes were temporarily reduced to one term only and to sleeping in the old 'D' block mess-room that had latterly been used as a cinema. In April 1940 Captain Cunliffe was appointed Naval Officer in Charge of the port of Dartmouth and the College became still more crowded as dormitories had to be converted into offices and a full operations room constructed. WRNS officers and ratings also began to appear for the first time.

Kempson retired in 1942 to be succeeded by J W Stork from Portsmouth Grammar School. His first term had not started when the College was bombed on 18th September. The damage was quite severe and it was necessary to send the junior cadets to Muller's Orphanage in Bristol, commissioned as HMS *Bristol*. Only the four senior terms of RNC cadets returned to Dartmouth but the Admiralty decided to use the buildings as a Combined Operations training centre. After a year as such, first as HMS *Dartmouth II* and then as HMS *Effingham*, the establishment was passed to the U.S. Navy as an advanced base.

By February 1943 HMS *Britannia* had re-assembled at Eaton Hall, the Duke of Westminster's impressive house near Chester, to remain there until the summer of 1946. The return to Dartmouth was delayed by the need to repair the bomb damage and the opportunity was also taken to improve the College buildings. The library was doubled in size, the science laboratories were expanded and a new 'F' block was begun to provide extra classrooms.

A system of scholarships to Dartmouth had been introduced in 1941 but they did not go far enough to widen the college entry. The Admiralty announced, therefore, that from September 1948 cadets were to enter Dartmouth at sixteen. This was the age that many boys of the required qualifications left state secondary schools and it removed the advantage that private-sector boys had in applying to enter Dartmouth at the natural break-point in their education. In any case, it was felt that thirteen was too early an age to choose a career and to be able to detect whether a candidate had the right qualities to become an officer. Fees for boarding and tuition would be abolished. The 'Special Entry' would continue at Dartmouth alongside the 'Sixteen Entry'. Thirteen-year-olds would still join RNC until May 1949.

The end of the younger entry caused the number of 'Darts' to decline as the extra sixteen-year-olds did not make up for the loss of the junior terms. The low birth rate of the 1930s was limiting the number of suitable candidates but the new age of entry presented particular problems as the headmasters of public and grammar schools became increasingly reluctant to lose boys in the middle of their school careers. By the summer term of 1953, at the end of which the last thirteen entries passed out, the College was down to 202 'Darts' and 45 'Benbows'. There were only four houses, Blake, Exmouth, Grenville and St Vincent and both 'C' and 'F' blocks were closed, the newest building after only very brief use. These buildings had been used by the Benbows who had moved up the hill in 1950 to be more closely integrated with the rest of the College. The following year their old barracks had been taken over by HMS *Hawke*, the training establishment for 'Upper Yardmen', young officer candidates from the lower deck.

The Admiralty had recognised that the existing cadet entry situation was most unsatisfactory and, in July 1952, a 'Committee on Cadet Entry' had been appointed under the chairmanship of the Hon Ewen Montague, Judge Advocate of the Fleet. This duly reported, in April 1954, in favour of restoring a thirteen entry at Dartmouth which would be converted into something much more like a normal boarding school with the Headmaster in charge under the supervision of the Rear Admiral, Admiralty Interview Board. Boys would still be able to enter at sixteen, and the Special Entry at eighteen would be retained, indeed the latter would be confirmed as the major source of officers.

Mr F Barraclough, the Chief Education Officer for the North Riding of Yorkshire, disagreed so fundamentally with these recommendations that he wrote his own minority report. This recommended retaining the sixteen entry but argued in favour of an eventual move to an all-eighteen entry when practicable. This was the natural break in a young man's education, especially given the contemporary trend to staying on at school. Barraclough did not think the time was yet ripe for such a change but the Admiralty disagreed and decided to go ahead and make it immediately. When the 'Committee on Officer Structure and Training' (COST) was set up at the beginning of 1954 under the chairmanship of Vice Admiral Sir Aubrey Mansergh, its first and most urgent task was to design a new 'Eighteen Entry' training scheme.

In its initial report presented in March, COST welcomed the end of the old Dartmouth scheme and argued that all officers could now be given a comprehensive professional training before going to sea. Dartmouth should become a 'Naval Academy' with an attached training squadron where officers could undertake a twenty-eight month course before going to sea as midshipmen. This would begin with a two-term academic 'levelling' process to cover deficencies in scientific knowledge or self-expression abilities. After the weaker cadets had been weeded by examinations the rest would proceed to the Dartmouth Training Squadron where they would serve as the ships' companies to get sea experience and knowledge of lower-deck conditions of service. They would then return to Dartmouth for four terms' professional instruction, reinforced by further education in academic subjects, short courses in the DTS and a visit to a naval air station. It was subsequently decided to promote cadets to midshipmen on completion of their squadron time and that they would go to sea as acting sub lieutenants. This amendment, which temporarily abolished the sea-going midshipman, was to help doom the scheme to a short life.

The new scheme was to begin in the summer of 1955 and at the end of the easter term, as the College prepared to celebrate its fiftieth anniversary, there was a distinct feeling that an era was ending. The 'Benbows' and 'Hawkes' would disappear, the former into the new scheme, the latter to a new establishment at South Queensferry. The existing sixteen entries would have to complete their education before moving into the COST scheme.

Twenty-five Years of Change

Dartmouth would have to be transformed for its new role. Dormitories had to be converted into single cabins for the midshipmen and four-berthers for the cadets to allow for study as well as sleeping. The gunroom accommodation also had to be improved to reflect the more relaxed atmosphere. The traditional classrooms were no longer adequate on their own and tutorial rooms were required to replace many of them. 'C' block was the first part of the College to be rebuilt and it was ready to receive the first 38 members of the new entry in May 1955. For the time being they were left separate in a new 'Drake Division' and the four houses continued as before for the sixteen entries.

The College in about 1919. 'D' block is complete, though the sick-bay has gained an extra storey since this photo was taken. The *Pomone* lies off Sandquay, but the destroyer ahead of her has defied identification. It is not *Sturgeon*. *(Photo National Maritime Museum)*.

The new scheme would require more staff, especially officers, to handle the technical professional instruction and the wardroom had to be extended. This pushed the victualling stores, which themselves had to be enlarged, out into a new block adjoining the west end of the College. Expanded naval and clothing stores also took over a wing of the hospital. A new gunnery block was begun and the neglected 'F' block became a well-equipped navigation and communications instruction building. The foundations were also laid for an annexe to 'D' block to contain cabins, tutorial rooms and new administrative offices. The 'Hawke' barracks was also modified for the expanded ships' company and became 'Beatty' Division.

Although the conversion to tertiary college was in principle more radical than the changes of 1905, the process was slow, gentle and more subtle. There was no question of replacing the academic staff. Mr Stork did, however, become 'Director of Studies' at the beginning of 1956 and his masters became lecturers. They were also now full members of the Wardroom Mess. 1956 also saw the end of the houses and the beginning of five new 'divisions' in which all the officers under training were integrated. The names were traditional:– Blake, Drake, Exmouth, Grenville and St Vincent. The Dartmouth Training Squadron also became operational. By summer 1957 there were over five hundred officers under training at the new BRNC, 171 cadets and 419 midshipmen and these included young men from Australia, Ceylon, Malaya, New Zealand and Pakistan as well as Britain. The staff totalled 57 officers and 42 lecturers.

They were not, however, to be given the chance to settle down to the new scheme. The COST training was due for early review owing to another of the Committee's proposals, the setting-up of the 'General List' of officers from the various specialisations. A committee was duly appointed on 1st April 1958, chaired by Sir Keith Murray, Chairman of the University Grants Committee, and it reported on the 26th of September of the same year. Despite the fact that the 1955 scheme had barely begun and its products had not yet reached the fleet as fully qualified officers, the Committee felt it had too many defects and ought to be changed forthwith. Entrance standards were both too low and too variable. The close interweaving of academic and professional studies at BRNC gave insufficient time for proper development in either. The academic staff at Dartmouth was praised for its work in bringing the least able cadets up to standard but it was felt that the better cadets suffered and there was no external qualification to show for the course afterwards. The DTS time was not properly exploited and 'officer-like qualities' were being neglected, not only in the intellectual but in the character and leadership sense.

The Murray Committee would have liked to restore the old thirteen entry. Instead it put forward a radically changed 'eighteen entry' system. Firstly, the entrance qualifications would be increased to a minimum of two 'A' levels. To give a proper professional and 'C and L' grounding a whole cadet year would be concentrated on this at Dartmouth, including a term in DTS where proper instruction would be given. After a second year with the fleet at sea as a midshipman, the trainee would return to Dartmouth as an acting sub lieutenant for a year's academic course of first-year degree standard. The Committee specifically wished to keep Dartmouth which they praised for its traditions, situation and buildings. Most of all, however, they felt it lent itself to keeping all specialisations together for as long as possible in accordance with the new 'GL' concept. To satisfy London University whose external degree would be completed by the Engineers at RNEC Manadon, there might have to be a considerable expansion of the laboratories, not to mention a radical reorganisation and strengthening of the academic staff. Nevertheless there was enough room for the 370 cadets and sub lieutenants expected annually.

Although the suggested scheme was adopted in basics, not all the 'Murray' suggestions were put into effect exactly as planned. By the time the first cadet entry arrived in September 1960 there had been some significant changes. The most important was that the Engineers were not to come to Dartmouth for their third year, and this allowed the problems of external approval and validation to be avoided. Indeed CWE Ghey's appointment as Director of Studies in 1959 had stressed continuity of academic staff; he had first joined as a master in 1926.

The return of the 'Murray Scheme' sub lieutenants in September 1962 meant that the higher standard of academic teaching called for by the report could begin. The officers-under-training could now concentrate on it, their professional indoctrination being over, although the sub lieutenants' leadership would be consolidated and extended by their role in helping run the College. The independence of the academic course from external examinations was turned to advantage as it allowed flexible mixtures of navally-orientated academic subjects to evolve. The new stress on tutorials and private study was in the finest traditions of Ewing and Ashford, albeit now at a higher level.

Although the 'Murray Scheme' was the main College task of the 1960s, that decade saw a great increase in the number of different entries coming to the College and different courses offered to them. The Royal Marine Young Officers Courses of one term's introduction to the Navy were carried out in DTS rather than the College following the new scheme's introduction but the 'Upper Yardmen' returned from their northern exile in HMS *Temeraire* in 1960. They took up residence in the hospital which had ceased to operate as such in 1958 and had been used since by the Admiralty Interview Board. The course lasted two years before they went to sea as midshipmen. The 'Temeraires' were integrated with the other five divisions two years later. 1960 had also seen the start of a new Supplementary List Aircrew entry who began to come to Dartmouth for a two-term combined professional and academic course before flying training. The Supplementary List was extended to Seamen in 1961 with a course of similar length at the college plus a term in DTS before proceeding to the fleet as midshipmen. They were later joined by SL Engineer officers who did the first two terms of the Dartmouth course before proceeding to Manadon. Instructor officers-under-training (IOUTs) began to attend Dartmouth for a one-term naval training course in 1962. That year also saw the beginning of a special course for 'New Commonwealth' and foreign officers who were beginning to come to the College in increasing numbers. At first a 'New Commonwealth Year' was offered instead of the RN Academic course, which could also be done by Commonwealth and foreign officers if sufficiently qualified and 'Internationals' were also entered in the SL Seaman Scheme. By 1967, however, a special package had been devised for all these officers with a term's academic work in their third cadet term and an 'International Senior Term' of more advanced study.

By the mid 1960s the College contained almost 700 officers-under-training and the staff comprised 54 officers and 34 lecturers. It was again divided into five divisions, a new 'Hawke' having been re-born in the hospital buildings in 1963 to concentrate the SL (Air) entry. The year after, however, it became a division like the others. Other new names which appeared were 'Cunningham' which replaced 'Exmouth' as a divisional title in 1968 and 'Jellicoe' which replaced 'Grenville' at the same time. Numbers began to decline once more, however, and even in a busy winter term there were only 477 OUTs in the College by 1970. Drake Division was therefore abolished, yet again, at the end of that year's summer term.

One reason for this decline and a factor that was by then threatening the College's very existence as an academic institution was the move towards a graduate entry. The 1960s was the decade of expansion in higher education associated with the Robbins report and the Services felt that they would lose the very best officer candidates if they did not follow this trend. In 1963 the first five cadets were nominated to go to university instead of doing the Dartmouth third year. In September 1964 'Seaman Officers Under Training' arrived at Dartmouth to inaugurate what later became known as the 'Direct Graduate Entry' (DGE) scheme. In 1965 the 'University Cadet Entry' (UCE) was begun whereby boys leaving school with university places would take them up sponsored by the Navy. On graduation they would do professional training at Dartmouth together with a course in technological subjects for arts graduates.

It seemed to some, however, that service education needed a more fundamental shake-up in the era of both an expanded graduate entry and the moves to greater unification of the armed forces. In 1966 in a thorough-going study of service education, Michael Howard, Professor of War Studies at King's College London and Mr Cyril English, Senior Chief Inspector, Department of Education and Science came to the conclusion that new entry academic instruction should be centralised at a Royal Defence College where the top 20% of candidates would read for degrees. This appealed to Mr Healey, the defence minister, and the scheme was adopted and announced in the 1967 Defence White Paper. Plans were made to establish the institution on the site of the Royal Military College of Science at Shrivenham. The scheme was subjected to considerable criticisms but it finally grounded on the rocks of financial stringency and the emergency defence cuts of 1967–8. It seemed, though, that when H G Stewart, a member of the science staff since 1947, was appointed Dartmouth's Director of Studies in September 1967 he might well be the last.

Although the College survived the abortive Howard-English exercise it was almost immediately under a fresh attack. The Defence White Paper of 1968 had stated that possible ways of giving officers degree standard academic training would continue to be investigated. The Navy now proposed to begin at Greenwich a course run by City University which would be attended by all Seamen and Supply sub lieutenants instead of the Dartmouth third year. At the end of this period the best students would go on to complete a full degree course at City while the others would pass on to further training courses as usual. Civilians would join with the naval officers. This threatened to reduce the College to an initial training establishment without both its senior officers under training and its best academic staff and was strongly opposed.

Although this battle was eventually won the tide was running too strongly against the 'Murray Scheme' for it to survive. Trust was placed in the UCE scheme to provide an increasing number of officers but to supplement it a new 'Naval College Entry' was being mooted by 1971. Officers-under-training of all three branches would come to Dartmouth to do a common period of 'Naval General Training' of a professional and 'Character and Leadership' type. One term would be taken in the College and another in a Dartmouth Training Ship. After that they would split up. Engineers would go to Manadon or Cambridge and some qualified Seamen and Supply officers-under-training with no university places would be 'nominated', either to City for the RN-sponsored 'Systems and Management' course or to another university. The General List 'non graduate' would go on to two terms of academic instruction at BRNC and the SL Seamen and Supply officers to one term. As many UCEs as possible would be encouraged to defer going up to university so that they might do the Naval General Training course first at Dartmouth. The other entries' training would not be changed very much although they would have to fit in with the new syllabus and timing. In 1972 as a sign of the new system all the junior officers under training became midshipmen and the rank of 'Cadet' was abolished after 128 years. The Naval College Entry course has seen a little evolution too; a more intensive four-week period of introductory training was introduced in the mid 70s while the General List academic course has been extended to three terms.

Until the 1970s Dartmouth remained an all-male bastion, at least as far as students were concerned, but the advent of two-week and four-week Short Introductory Courses for doctors, nurses, dentists, chaplains and instructors brought about a change. The course of QARNNS in Spring 1973 had the distinction of being the first women officers-under-training at BRNC. They were soon followed by lady dentists and doctors and female constructors. In 1976 the WRNS decided to confirm this co-educational policy by transferring their officer training course of one term's professional and academic work to Dartmouth from Greenwich. They form a separate 'Talbot' division.

By September 1978 when C H Christie became BRNC's fourth Director of Studies the varied look of today's College was very apparent in the list of officers-under-training. The Senior Gunroom was made up of 297 OUTs: 48 General List NCE, 45 Supplementary List (Air), 40 International Midshipmen, 40 Graduated UCEs, 29 Direct Graduate Entries, 16 IOUTs, 15 Senior International Term, 14 'St George' candidates, 14 WRNS OTC, 12 Supplementary List NCE and 11 Royal Marine Officers. Of these less than half were on purely academic courses. Also doing professional training were the 196 juniors:– 136 GL NCEs, 31 'Deferred' UCEs, 23 SL (Air) and 6 SL NCE. Nothing could better illustrate that balance at BRNC between academic and professional instruction has swung firmly in favour of the latter. The staff figures reflected this too with only 32 lecturers but over 60 officers. With so many of the College's courses now lasting only one term, the atmosphere had altered fundamentally compared with the more leisurely pace of ten years previously. Now that most new naval officers did their long-term academic work at university, in September 1978 there were 136 UCEs and 57 nominations.

This is the Britannia Royal Naval College which enters its seventy-fifth anniversary year and it can look forward to still more changes. The buoyant recruiting figures look like pushing numbers of officers-under-training to approaching 800. A new very short-career commission which has just been announced will mean yet another new entry and course. Long-promised modernisation may actually take place. With one or two trivial exceptions every RN officer passes through BRNC on one course or other. The College's aims, the inculcation of a broad view of the naval profession, the development of the conduct and sense of duty required of an officer and the preparation of officers for further training, remain what they always have been. They are grounded in three-quarters of a century of tradition, for change at Dartmouth is always tempered by stability. Ewing and Ashford could not stamp out the old *Britannia* entirely and several features of BRNC's way of life still go back to 1905 if not before. Indeed, even when they planned the great upheaval of that year, the architects of the new scheme recognised that although times were changing, the best of the old traditions had to be combined with the creation of new. As social and technological development has speeded up, their successors have had to grapple with the problem of coming up with the optimum synthesis of these two conflicting forces. Dartmouth has therefore always been evolving, sometimes in new directions, but always retaining a distinctive aura of its own.

CHAPTER 1

Genesis and Early Development

The first training ship at Dartmouth was the 4th ship of the Royal Navy to be called *Britannia*. She was a wooden three-decked ship-of-the-line, which had been launched in 1820, but not modernized with steam engines, although she had taken part in the Crimean War. She was the successor to the third *Britannia*, which had carried the flag of the Earl of Northesk at the battle of Trafalgar. She had replaced HMS *Illustrious* as a cadet training ship at Portsmouth in 1859, and had moved to Portland in February 1862.

Here she is seen just after moving to the Dart, where she lay between 1863 and 1869, providing a static training ship for new-entry officers. Although the old two-decker, HMS *Hindostan* was brought in to provide additional accommodation in 1864, she proved too small and unhealthy, and was replaced. *(Photograph is one of a stereo pair taken by Cranford of Dartmouth, Canon M Kennedy collection)*.

Basic officer-training facilities for the Royal Navy were provided by the fifth HMS *Britannia* (left) and the third HMS *Hindostan*, from 1869 to 1905. The fifth *Britannia* started life as the *Prince of Wales*, a wooden three-decked ship-of-the-line, launched in Portsmouth Dockyard on 25th January, 1860 after twelve years on the stocks. She was obsolete when launched, as the first British iron-clad, HMS *Warrior*, was already being built. The *Prince of Wales* never served at sea as a warship; instead she was brought to Dartmouth and renamed *Britannia* on 3rd March, 1869. The *Hindostan* was a two-decked ship-of-the-line, launched in Plymouth Dockyard on 8th August, 1841, brought to Dartmouth in 1864, transferred to Plymouth in 1905, where she became part of the Artificer training establishment as *Fisgard III*, and finally broken up in 1921, thus outlasting the fifth *Britannia* by five years. The two ships were linked by a gangway, floating under which can be seen a sort of black tank. This was the cadets' winter swimming pool, and was heated by a steam-pipe from the *Britannia*. The summer swimming pool is the white rectangle visible between the fore and mainmasts of HMS *Wave*, which is lying alongside the port-side of the *Hindostan*. The *Wave*, a wooden steam tender which began life as the *Edeline*, was purchased by the Admiralty in 1882. She was originally barque-rigged, and used for sail and steam training.

The site of the future college can be seen, the eastern end of the present building being in the patch of grass to the left of and slightly beyond the white-walled enclosure. *(Photo College Archive)*.

The figurehead of the *Britannia* which is still to be seen on the College parade ground. This photograph was taken from the stern of the *Hindostan* in about 1903–4. This figurehead can also be seen in the photograph of the fourth *Britannia*, whence it was taken on renaming. *(Photo Cdr HP Mead collection, I.W.M.).*

Two drawings of the future college: the lower one appeared in the Britannia Magazine for Easter 1899, and the upper (the original of which now hangs outside the Captain's office) was printed in the Army & Navy Illustrated for 24th June, 1899. This picture is by Sir Aston Webb, 1849–1930, who was the architect of the College. The lower picture probably represents an earlier sketch as there are some obvious differences from the eventual building. The upper picture more closely resembles the final design. The layout of the present parade ground, intended and built as a front garden, is completely different. The earlier sketch gives the impression of a flat site.

The new College begins to take shape on Mount Boone in the summer of 1900. The ramps, the foundations of the Captain's house and the retaining wall in front of the wardroom are well under way, but work on the College buildings proper appears hardly to have started. *(Photo Army & Navy Illustrated, 8th September, 1900; N.M.M.).*

Dartmouth and Kingswear from somewhere near the Castle in the summer of 1900. The new College can be seen being built and the two ships are visible, lying off Sandquay. In the foreground are the Imperial German Navy Cruisers *Irene* & *Gefion*. German warships were quite frequent visitors to Dartmouth before the development of the new German navy caused Britain to abandon 'splendid isolation' in favour of the 'Entente Cordiale' and better relations with France. *(Courtesy of Mrs K Willett).*

These three pictures show more of the building of the College. The top one is taken from the bank beyond the west end of the main building and the corridor running away from the photographer is that which presently divides the senior gunroom from the wardroom. This photograph, along with the others, was published in the Navy and Army Illustrated for 8th March, 1902, but evidently was taken long before the foundation stone laying on 7th March. Probably they were taken in the summer of 1901. It is striking how much more advanced the hospital or sick quarters are (centre). The unhealthiness of the old ships was a major reason behind the decision to bring the cadets ashore, and, in fact, the hospital, which now houses Hawke division and the naval stores, was opened long before the new college was complete. The hospital was built much closer to the site proposed for the college in 1875 than was eventually the choice in 1898. There appear to be no surviving signs of the inclined plane (bottom). *(N.M.M.)*.

Two more views of building operations taken around 1901–2. In the first the kitchen block occupies the foreground with the present senior gunroom clearly visible to the right. Running back from this, the main corridor is becoming recognisable. In the second, the present quarterdeck area begins to take shape. *(College Archive)*.

On 7th March, 1902, King Edward VII (incidentally the last king not to be educated at Dartmouth), came to the construction site of the new 'Britannia Royal Naval College' to lay the foundation stone of the main building, although work on the site had actually begun in 1898. The first picture shows the interior of the impressive 120-foot-by-36-foot wooden pavilion erected for the occasion. The drapery lining the walls was red and white. In the second can be seen the foundation stone itself, after laying, and part of the mechanism used for lowering the stone into position. This was a chain and wire operated from outside the pavilion, with a voicepipe communicating the orders. The inscription on the foundation stone was on a gilded background which has since disappeared. The drawings of the college as it was to look after completion are also visible. The Marine's name was Somers. *(Higgs & Hill, which company built the College).*

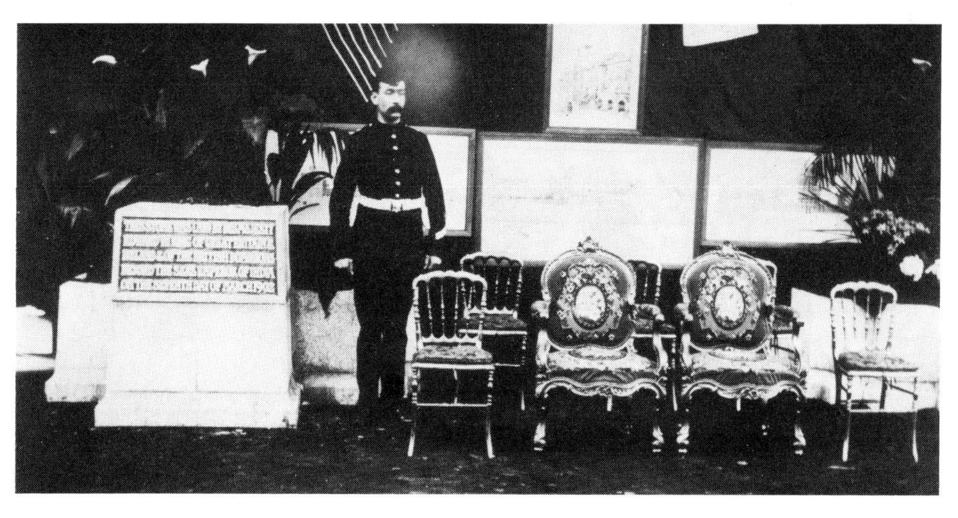

The sick quarters as completed: their large size reflected the contemporary problems, particularly with infectious diseases. Although immediately after the new hospital's opening in September 1902, there was a sudden improvement in the health of the cadets, the usual epidemics soon reappeared. This picture shows the front facing the Dart. Sometimes the diseases were fatal, as for example in the case of Cadet Boycott, whose funeral cortege is shown leaving the front of the sick quarters, after he died there on 11th June, 1904. The carriage is standing outside the east end of the hospital, now Hawke Division. The house on the left, now occupied by the Commander of the College, was built for the Medical Officer. *(Photos College Archive, (J S Ward))*.

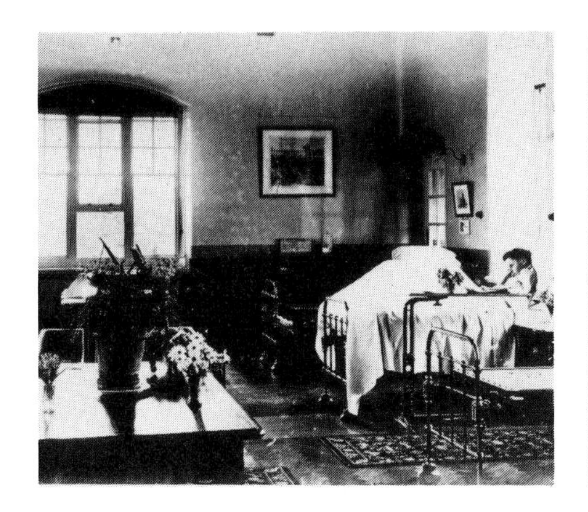

Left A ward in the sick quarters as built, with a cadet enjoying comparative peace and quiet, probably in the summer of 1905. The cadet cannot escape naval character-building influences. The print on the far wall is 'The Boyhood of Raleigh'. *Right* This magnificent period-piece of a room is the drawing room in the doctor's house. He does seem to escape naval uplift amidst all this glorious clutter. *(Photos College Archive)*.

By this time, around 1903, the new College was recognisable. It was clear that its role would be different from that intended and that the original design was inadequate before completion. *(College Archive)*.

As a first step towards the building, the playing fields were extended and improved, during the winter 1898–9. Here we see them in 1905 during the annual Assault-at-Arms. This was a mixture of bayonet drill, boxing, and gymnastics. Although the tower of the nearly complete college is visible in the background, none of the boys taking part was allowed to see the inside. It had been decided that cadets who had been under training in the ships would contaminate the cadets of the new scheme with the vices of the old. *(Photo Dalrymple-Hamilton Collection)*.

HMS *Eclipse*, name-ship of her class, a 5600-ton second-class protected cruiser, built in Portsmouth and completed in 1897. She embarked the fifty cadets of what would have been the third term of the Britannia scheme and took them to Bermuda where they completed the normal 'school' part of their training. The junior term embarked in HMS *Highflyer*, a similar ship, but completed in 1899, with three funnels due to her Belleville boilers. *Highflyer* remained in Bermuda for two terms. *(Photo Dalrymple-Hamilton Collection)*.

Although of poor quality, these two photographs, taken by one of the cadets, illustrate the training in Bermuda. One shows the *Eclipse* and the *Highflyer* alongside, while the other shows the facilities ashore, which comprised four classrooms, a physical science laboratory, a drawing instruction room, and a gymnasium. *(Photos Dalrymple-Hamilton Collection)*.

After their time in Bermuda the Britannia cadets passed on to the cruiser *Isis*. She is here seen lying in the Dart. *Isis* made her last training cruise in the Easter term of 1907. *(Photo Mrs K. Willett)*.

A general view of Dartmouth, with the new college standing out, perhaps a little brashly, and before the additions of later years altered its front aspect. *(Picture Courtesy of David Sherrard)*.

The Selborne scheme necessitated two major additions, the construction of a new wing begun in 1903 to house two extra terms, and the addition in 1905 of a substantial mansion for the Headmaster. This is Aston Webb's drawing of the Headmaster's house. The structure on the left of the drawing is the end of the extra wing, now known as 'C' block. *(Drawing, now in the College Collection, by courtesy of the Rev R H Horne, who is the first headmaster's grandson).*

The front of the College as built, looking towards the Captain's house. *(Photo College Archive).*

This photograph, shows the west side of the centre block, and the back of 'A' block. *(Photo College Archive).*

The cadets' mess room. The 'electroliers' in the form of sailing ships are still there, and the medallions on the ceiling have recently been painted for the first time. *(Photo College Archive).*

The wardroom anteroom. *(Photo College Archive)*.

'The Bathing Lake', with, in the background, the gymnasium. The pool was little more complete than this when opened the next year. The contemporary *Britannia Magazine* reported 'a good deal of discomfort in dressing and undressing, and much good Devonshire soil is taken into the bath on the feet of cadets.' The bath was roofed over by summer 1907. *(Photo College Archive)*.

The seamanship room. *(Photo College Archive).*

The College officers, masters and cadets in July 1906. The Captain, W E Goodenough, is in the centre of the front row with the first Headmaster, Mr Cyril Ashford, on his right. Present in this photograph are the first three terms of the Selborne scheme cadets and the last two terms of the Britannia scheme. *(Photo College Archive).*

The chapel in 1909. The chapel took longer to complete than any other part of the original college, because, while the Admiralty paid for the basic building, the decorations were paid for by public subscription. This photograph shows the reredos after all seven statues had been put in position, but before the communion rail was brought across. *(Photo College Archive, Evan-Thomas Collection).*

The commissioning of the new pre-dreadnought battleship, HMS *Britannia*, in 1906, necessitated a change of the College's name. In 1905 *Hindostan* had been moved to Devonport, and her berth was taken by HMS *Espiegle*, an almost new but completely obsolete sloop which was used as a mobile tender. In the summer of 1906 the sloop became the ship upon whose books the personnel of the College were borne. *(Photo Radio Times Hulton Picture Library).*

The Main Hall or Quarterdeck, 1909–1911. The models have, sadly, been lost. They are of, left, HMS *Calliope*, a steel corvette of 1884, and HMS *Black Prince*, the Royal Navy's second ironclad, of 1862. The glass case in the centre housed a piece of silver plate which once belonged to Nelson. *(Photo College Archive. Evan-Thomas Collection)*.

In January 1910 *Espiegle* was replaced by the third-class protected cruiser *Pomone*, completed in 1899. When she was hulked for service at Dartmouth, she lost her forefunnel, and is here seen forward of the old *Britannia*, which was used as ratings' quarters until her sale to Garnhams on 13th November, 1914. *(Picture courtesy of Lady Serpell)*.

'MOBILIZE.' Such was the telegram received by Captain Stanley at 3.50 p.m. on 1st August, 1914. By 10.46 p.m. the last of three special trains carrying the cadets and their chests and 200 of the ship's company had left Kingswear for Portsmouth, Chatham and Devonport. This photograph shows the cadets packing up on that fateful day. *(Photo College Archive).*

The expansion of the Navy, even before the outbreak of the First World War, had led to plans for a doubling of the intake of potential officers. This made extra accommodation at Dartmouth necessary, and three larger gunrooms and other facilities were begun during the summer term of 1914. The opportunity was taken to rectify some of the omissions in the original design. It had already been necessary to add extra classrooms and a reference library when the present 'E' block was built in 1906–7. It had then been possible to build the single-storey block without marring the effect of Aston Webb's original plan. The even newer block, however, could not be hidden. It is, effectively, a three-storey building whose ground floor is on the same level as the top floor of the main college. It thus destroyed the original skyline, and, being a rather stark rectangular building, made of a different grade of brick, it has done nothing for the college's looks. These three views, opposite and overleaf top, show 'D' block (as it is now called) under construction during the War; the older single-storey 'Reference Library Block' can be clearly seen behind the steam engine in the third picture and to the right is visible the original back wall of the College building *(Photo, College Archive).*

The old hulk *Britannia* was resold to Hughes Bolckow, and was finally towed away early in July 1916. 'The whole College was assembled to watch her passing, whilst the band paid her the last farewell, and furtive expression was not infrequently heard of a feeling that an enemy torpedo would be a not unfitting end to her career of usefulness.' *(Britannia Magazine*, 1916.) *(Photo College Archive)*.

A term gunroom, thought to be that of St. Vincent term of May 1917, which suddenly became the senior term when the three older terms were sent to sea during the summer. This is one of the four gunrooms in the original building. *(Photo Imperial War Museum).*

Sheep grazing above the west end of the College, probably in the early spring of 1917. The 'sky studies' are complete. *(Photo Imperial War Museum).*

One of the eight dormitories in the original building, possibly one on the top floor of the building. Each dormitory was named after a famous admiral. The cadets are standing by their traditional sea chests, in which all their possessions were kept. *(Photo Imperial War Museum).*

CHAPTER 2

The Calm Before the Second Storm

A quiet summer's day sailing in a sloop-rigged cutter. The summer is that of 1930 and the College is going about the job of producing naval officers. The 1920's and 1930's were the longest period of relative stability in the College's history. This 'halcyon' period was far too short. It ran from the end of the First World War to the beginning of the Second, a period of almost exactly twenty years, or, more accurately in the College's case, from 1921 when the two establishments at Dartmouth and Osborne were merged, until a very successful Royal Visit on 22nd and 23rd July, 1939, rang down the curtain on the old College and the old naval world forever. *(Photo College Archive)*.

The pattern of life and instruction changed little after 1921. The photographs in this chapter seek to illustrate that life. Seamanship was always important. On page 39 is a photograph of the seamanship room in 1905. It is not in the space marked for it on the plans of the College in 1905, which was the area to the north of the Quarterdeck, including the two passages leading up to 'D' block and the bookstore nowadays, but is the space above, the area now used as the science laboratory preparation room and the present corridors. The photograph in chapter one shows the south-east corner of that space. The picture below shows the space below, which was where the original plans put the seamanship room, in 1917–18. The half-hull models behind the cadets have a horrible irony. They are, from the top, the armoured cruisers *Monmouth*, *Cressy*, and *Drake*, all sunk during the First World War, the first two taking a lot of the cadets who had been mobilized in August 1914 with them. Opposite, top, shows the new seamanship room, in a glass-roofed space in the extension linking the old building to 'D' block. The picture was taken early in 1931. Much of the same instructional equipment is visible as in 1905, notably the forecastle model, centre left behind the table. Also visible is a model of the large light cruiser *Glorious* before her conversion to an aircraft carrier, continuing the collection of ill-fated ships. Opposite middle, taken in the autumn of 1931, shows the same room, with the new forecastle model of HMS *Rodney*. Just poking out from behind the head of the second cadet from the left is a model of the aircraft carrier *Eagle*, which fits nicely into the series of sunken ships. Opposite bottom shows the same room on 27th October, 1939. The only real change is that the cadets have their gasmasks with them. The instructor is Mr Fleet. *(Photo Page 48 Imperial War Museum). (Photos page 49 Top College Archive Middle and Bottom Radio Times Hulton Picture Library).*

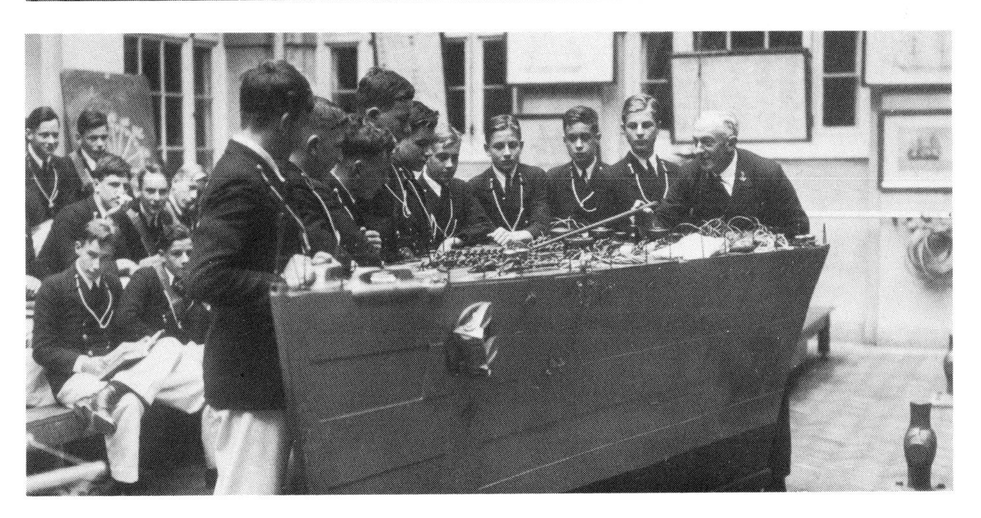

Seamanship was not limited to the classroom or even to the river. From 1919 to 1925 HMS *Sturgeon*, an Admiralty 'R' class destroyer of 1065 tons, built by Stephen and completed on 26th February 1917, provided facilities for practical training. This picture shows her lying at her buoys in the Dart in the summer of 1919, probably July. *(Photo Dalrymple-Hamilton Collection)*.

In September 1925 the *Sturgeon* was replaced by HMS *Forres*, and sent for disposal. The *Forres* was a later Hunt Class Minesweeper built as the *Fowey*, launched, after renaming, by the Clyde Shipbuilding Co. on 22 November 1918, and thus completed too late to participate in the war. This 800-ton, twin-screw vessel, with neither guns nor torpedo tubes, and with only 2,200 h.p. giving a speed of 16 knots, must have been much less exciting than *Sturgeon*'s 3–4 inch guns, 4–21 inch torpedo tubes and 27,000 h.p. Dalrymple-Hamilton recorded in his diary on 4th April, 1919, 'Took Joanie, Gwen, and Nana out in *Sturgeon*. We had all three kettles alight and went for another run on the measured mile at Slapton. Got 31.5 knots but did not force anything.' However the *Forres* took cadets on a series of week-long cruises. The *Forres*'s first captain, while at Dartmouth, was E S F Fegen who was to win undying fame in command of HMS *Jervis Bay* in 1940, when she fought the *Scheer* in defence of convoy HX 84. The *Forres* left Dartmouth in the summer of 1932, was sold for scrap in 1935 and was not replaced. This photograph was taken in the summer of 1931. *(Photo College Archive)*.

There was one major change on the river early in the period. The *Pomone* was towed away in December 1922, top. It was therefore necessary to commission a new ship on whose books the officers and men could be borne. The solution was to commission a small steam boat, which appears to have come from Osborne, and which was renamed *Britannia*. She is visible in the background at the right of the lower picture. In the foreground is a pulling gig. This photograph was taken at the time of the College Regatta in 1930. *(Photos College Archive).*

The River Dart was very important to the College life, but unlike today, it was only 'open' for about half the year.

Until May 1937 the College worked on the term system. Each group of cadets joining together did everything as a unified term. They were all very much the same age. The regulations between the wars meant that the entrance exam could only be taken once, between the ages of 13 years 4 months and 13 years 8 months. The term lived, worked, and relaxed together. The junior terms lived in the new block, each having a dormitory and a gunroom of its own. This picture shows Troubridge dormitory in 1930. The beds are arranged with their heads alternately towards the wall and towards the chests in which the cadets kept their possessions. In January 1930, it was rumoured among the cadets that a new rule was about to be introduced. The Term Cadet Captain of Hawke Term recorded it in his diary thus, 'In future anyone who wants to see a fellow from a junior term must put in a chit, to be signed by (his term officer) and the fellow's officer, after which at an appointed hour they enter the Q(uarter) D(eck) from opposite ends and have 5 minutes conversation.' Cadet van de Kasteele called the idea 'barmy' and, it appears to have been simply a rumour, but it also appears only to be an extreme version of the segregation which was the norm in the College before the ending of the term system. Each term used its gunroom as a recreation space and a prep room. The terms moved round from the most junior room which was at the west end of the main corridor of 'D' block via 'C'-block gunroom, the seventh term gunroom, to the most senior which was at the west end of 'A' block, closest to the messroom. Opposite shows the fifth term gunroom, in 'D' block, in the winter of 1930–1. *(Photos College Archive)*.

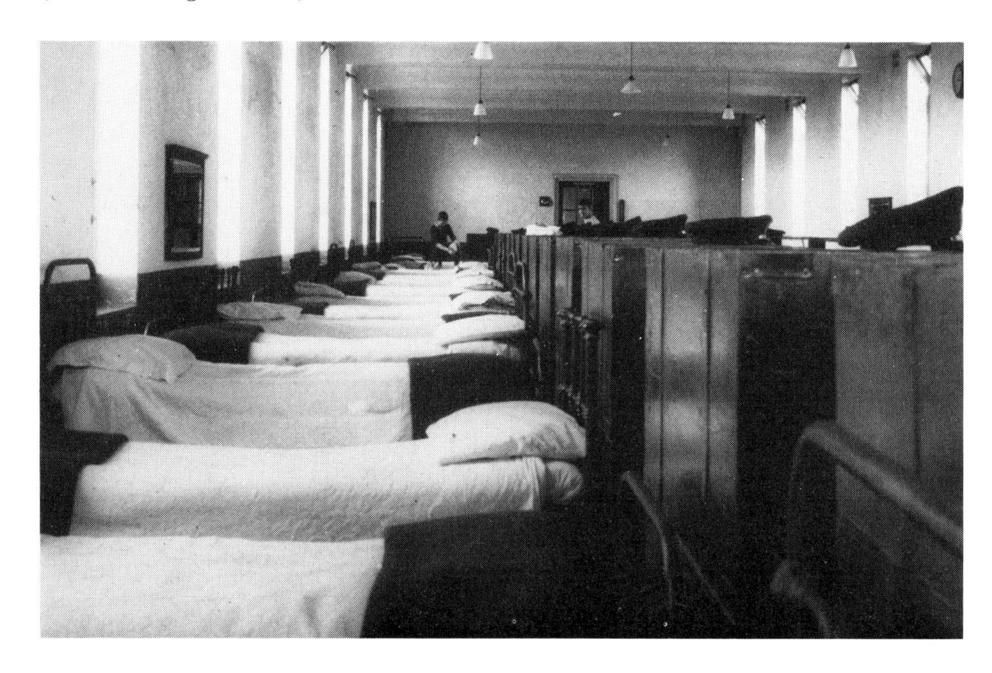

The picture below shows morning colours at weekday divisions sometime between 1929 and 1931, probably towards the end of that period. The position of the figurehead from the old *Britannia* is interesting. She has moved three times since she was taken from the ship. The College band is visible to the right of the mast. It was entirely made up of civilian College servants at this time. *(Photo College Archive)*.

For much of the interwar period there were two dining rooms for the cadets, as there are two to-day. (Top) The Junior messroom laid up for tea in 1930. Bottom shows the Senior messroom in the autumn of 1931. The doorway in the middle of the wall on the right has since been bricked up and panelled over. *(College Archive, Radio Times Hulton Picture Library).*

Divisions were held on the terraces in the front of the College. Originally they were held in amongst the bushes and grass of the front, as can clearly be seen in this picture taken about the end of the First World War. These are Sunday Divisions and it is an entirely uniformed affair. It only became the custom for the masters to attend later. After the war was over, the bushes were grubbed up, and, for a while, there seems to have been just a series of grass patches. They were removed in April 1926, when the present parade ground was laid out. *(Photo National Maritime Museum)*.

When the figurehead was removed from *Britannia* after her sale in 1914, she first came to rest part way up the steps from Sandquay. This photograph was taken towards the end of the First World War. *(Photo Imperial War Museum)*.

The engineering workshops were down at Sandquay, above, summer 1930, and a good part of the cadets' time was spent in them. In the timetable for the seventh term for May, 1942, twice as much time was allotted to engineering as seamanship. *(College Archive)*.

Cadet van de Kasteele records that in his sixth term, autumn 1929, he spent one quarter of his 'Sandquay time' in the drawing office, shown here in 1931. The officer is Captain S T Meyrick. *(Radio Times Hulton Picture Library)*.

One quarter of van de Kasteele's time was spent in the foundry, above at the end of the First World War, making moulds for valves and bearings, and half was spent in the machine shop, below in 1931, learning about lathes and other machines. *(Imperial War Museum and College Archive).*

Welding, above in 1939, and carpentry, below in 1917 or 1918, were also taught, and there was a fitting shop, opposite in 1931. This instruction, much of it by naval pensioners, was a bone of contention between naval and academic staffs. *(Radio Times Hulton Picture Library, Imperial War Museum and College Archive)*.

Ordinary school work formed the bulk of the cadet's activities. The timetable included thirty-two classes and five evening preparations, usually of fifty-five minutes each. The timetable of a cadet would change from term to term, but would run something like this at the end of our period for a new entry: Maths six classes and two preps, History three classes and one prep, French four classes and three preps, Science four periods with a prep every other week, English four classes with three preps in two weeks, Divinity one class, Gym two classes, Seamanship two, engineering two and revision prep one. The discrepancy between the numbers in that list and the totals above is because four preps were done during the ordinary instructional hours. By the end of a cadet's time, things would have changed a lot. Term Cadet Captain van de Kasteele, now in his tenth term, gives us the following account of Tuesday 25th March, 1930.

'Cross-country race to-day! Turn out 0635 and Navigation with Bish. My last prep turned out to be rather successful. Breakfast 0800 and Divisions 0900. The term had an exam, so got off.

From 0915 French Prep and Maths. Then Seamanship and History prep. At 1300 lunch. I ate far too much in view of this afternoon's job. The baked jam roll we had for pudding I couldn't resist, though Bill swore I'd be as sick as a dog.

Bank and belly muster. At 1415 I started for Norton with Glynn and Andrewes. Before we'd reached the Hospital the lorry passed us, with Robbie next the driver, so we leapt on board, thus being at any rate saved some fag before the actual race started, and got up to Norton about 1425.

The race was started by the Captain at 1445 and there was immediately a rush for the first hedge. There were fifty or sixty people in for it, but it was not long before they were all strung out.

I soon found out my error in eating that jam roll. Downhill as far as Venn but from there to the road it was a devilish grind, and for the last half of the run I had a vile stitch.

I finally got in about fifty yards behind two Rodneys. I thought I must be last, but actually I don't believe there were twenty people already in. It was a few moments before the next arrived, and still they kept coming in, so I didn't do too badly. (The picture below shows the finish of the 1931 cross-country. The photograph was taken by a cadet.)

Hastings won though he was literally foaming when he got in, and old Charlie Adams was only a few yards behind, which was grand. Glynn was third, and Gray about fifth.

. . . Of the dozen or so who did not finish, Andrewes was one. I don't blame them . . . for Hastings' time was, I think, a record. . . .

From 1620 Maths Prep and French. Supper 1830. Quarters and French prep. After rounds we had cocoa, etc. in the Messroom, and then Medd, Hunting, and I went over to Kimmins' (their term Officer) cabin. The old man was at home, with the portable wireless in full blast, so we listened and chatted . . . Did not get away till after 2230.' The phrase 'belly muster' refers to an inspection carried out by the Surgeon Lieutenant to check for signs of infectious diseases. Usually the cadets were called upon to display their stomachs while they were examined for rashes. Actually the epidemic going on in the spring of 1930 was mumps. On 27 March the diary records that the hospital was now full to overflowing and cadets were being cleared out of 'A' to make way for the unhealthy. *(College Archive.)*

In the summer of 1936, the mounting criticism of Dartmouth brought about the abandonment of the term system. The suggestion to do this seems to have come from the Admiralty, where the Second Sea Lord, Admiral Sir Martin Dunbar-Nasmith VC was an ex-captain of the College. The College authorities, Captain Reginald Holt, and Headmaster, E W Kempson, (left, Mr A G Piggott on right,) fell in with the idea. The new Captain, Frederick Dalrymple-Hamilton, appointed in January 1937, was quite clear that the new system was intended to make a 'public school'. *(Photo taken in 1931. Radio Times Hulton Picture Library).*

The new scheme required few physical alterations. They would not have been possible anyway. The whole of the changes excluding furnishings were costed at £1000 by the Captain, and he was told, by the C-in-C Plymouth, that there was no money in his control. In future there would be six houses; a new entry house called Drake situated in 'C' block. The picture below shows 'C' block on the left, in 1930, with 'B' block on the right and the chapel in between. The new entry would remain in Drake for two terms before moving on to one of the five ordinary houses, which were housed in 'A', 'B' and 'D' blocks. *(Photos College Archive).*

Each of the new houses was to have both officers and civilian academic staff attached, as has continued to the present day. There has, however, been a great expansion in the number of officers as courses have got shorter and naval training increased in importance.

While it was reported to the Admiralty that there had been a short-lived 'increase in immorality', the system worked well.

The College has always been a mecca for foreign service visitors, and amongst those at this time, were two officers from the Yugoslavian Navy. They seem to have suspected that they were not being shown everything, for they enquired after 'the College prison'.

In July 1938, one of the earliest combined-operations exercises was carried out when the Ninth Infantry Brigade was landed on Slapton Sands. The landing was a complete success but then, as prophesied by the navy, the weather broke and it was impossible for the troops to be re-embarked. The staff looked round for somewhere to put the men. Captain Dalrymple-Hamilton and the Britannia Magazine give considerable detail of how the College housed, fed, and then sent on their way 1300 officers and men of the King's Own Scottish Borderers and Lincolns. The only loss seems to have been one pair of Borderers' trews. The officers of the Brigade were very grateful for what had been done on the night 5–6 July and, as Dalrymple-Hamilton records in his diary, on 15th October, 1938, 'Brigadier B.L. Montgomery arrived in the evening with three officers from the 9th. Infantry Brigade to present a statuette of a modernly-equipped soldier as a mark of gratitude for our having put them all up . . . We had a small ceremony on QD which all the cadets attended. The Genl. made 'em a good speech on leadership and cooperation. Then handed over the statuette. The photographer failed with his flashlight photograph of this event. Then I said thank you and we dispersed. We all dined in the Wardroom and had a singsong which was great fun. Brigadier was promoted Major-General to-day and goes to Palestine.' The singsong does not sound very much like Monty's style, but the statuette is still to be seen on the main staircase. *(Photo C Risk).*

In the summer of 1939, there were some visitors, even more distinguished than the future victor of El Alamein, for the King, Queen and two Princesses visited the College 'privately' on 22 and 23 July. This visit has been the subject of considerable speculation, much of it ill-informed. What actually happened is, in outline at least, quite clear. It was a wet Saturday when the Royal Party arrived in the Royal Yacht. They came up to the Gymnasium, where they saw a gymnastics display. Then they watched a swimming display in the pool, after which they went down to the Quarter Deck, where some presentations were made. After that they planted some trees in the plot above the West End, and then had tea in the canteen. This was one of the most important pieces of building of the interwar period, having been completed in 1930. They then returned to the Yacht via Sandquay where they watched a sailing display including a race by twenty-one Dart One Design. There was a dinner aboard the Royal Yacht that night. On the Sunday morning, the King inspected Divisions, and presented prizes. After Chapel the King and Queen visited the sick quarters where they were cheered by the Cadets immured there with mumps or measles; there were epidemics of both that term. The Princesses had to be excluded from this and were entertained at the Captain's house. After lunch in the Captain's house, the Royal Party re-embarked and were followed out of the harbour by every boat, around 400, that the College possessed. The Captain went in one of the College's great prides, the yacht *Amaryllis*. She had been built in 1886 and had been sailed around the world between 1920 and 1923 by Lieutenant G H P Muhlhauser, RNVR. He had died shortly afterwards, and his sister had given her to the Navy for as long as she should be seaworthy. She arrived at Dartmouth in 1927, and gave yeoman service until 1951, when, in accordance with Miss Muhlhauser's wishes, she was towed out into Start Bay and sunk. Combined operations exercises were not the only portents of approaching war. The Munich crisis caused the cadets to fill sandbags and construct barriers round vulnerable windows. Exercises commenced in air raid precautions, which revealed an area of deficiency, in the original College design for which the architect could not be justly blamed. The heating ducts proved unsuitable as air raid shelters.

The Captain also had to make arrangements for the siting of machine guns on the roof of 'D' Block, though it was not until after the bombing of the College in September 1942, that anti-aircraft defences in the Dartmouth area were to reach a reasonable standard.

In the spring of 1939, HMS *Frobisher* had to be withdrawn from her role as training ship for the special or public school entry cadets, and it was necessary to accommodate them in the College for the first time. Care had to be taken about the introduction of the special entry to the College, for there had been clear signs of tension between the two types of cadets aboard the training cruiser *Vindictive*. Originally they were housed in the seamen's barracks, and the College worked a staggered routine, with two sittings for meals, two morning chapel services and two lots of divisions. Amongst the special entry cadets for the summer term of 1939 was Prince Philip of Greece, who was allowed to play a major part in hosting the visiting Princesses, as his uncle, Captain the Lord Louis Mountbatten, was present as the King's aide-de-camp. As the *Victoria and Albert* left the Dart, the King sent a message to the Captain telling him to announce an extra four days leave for the cadets to be added to the end of the summer holidays. This announcement was met by a storm of cheering, but the cadets were not to celebrate their good fortune in peace, for, before the College reassembled, war had come. That happy royal visit was the College's last carefree moment, and, although the same basic system of training was recommenced in September 1946, all was to change in the harsher post-war world.

HMY *Victoria and Albert* passing Dartmouth Castle on 22 July 1939. *(Western Morning News)*.

The gymnasium in 1930 (above) where the royal party saw a display like that below. This photograph actually shows the Hood term, then the second term, in the autumn of 1931. *(College Archive and Radio Times Hulton Picture Library)*.

The swimming pool in 1918. The roof to the swimming pool was completed well after the remainder of the original College *(Imperial War Museum)*.

The canteen in 1930. This building was one of the few major pieces of building in the interwar period, and it is shown immediately after completion, and before the yacht *Britannia*'s mast was erected as a flag-pole in May 1937. *(College Archive)*.

A Dart-one-design dinghy, crewed by Cadet T B Smeal in 1931. *(College Archive)*.

The King presenting sports trophies at Divisions, 23 July 1939. To the King's right is Commander C T Addis, Commander of the College, and beyond him Admiral Sir M Dunbar-Nasmyth, C-in-C Plymouth. Behind the King is Captain the Lord Louis Mountbatten, to the King's left are Captain F H Dalrymple-Hamilton, an unidentified Commander, possibly called Campbell, and a Cadet Captain, possibly D R Johnston, the Chief Cadet Captain. *(W Peek)*.

The College hospital 1930. *(College Archive)*.

The yacht '*Amaryllis*' on the slipway for cleaning about 1930. *(College Archive)*.

CHAPTER 3

The War Years and Eaton Hall

Every effort was made to keep the usual routine going in the College when the War started in 1939. The most conspicuous change was that many of the civilians donned uniform, at least in the Home Guard. This is the staff of the College in the Autumn of 1941. The Captain R L B Cunliffe is in the centre of the front row, with the Headmaster, E W E Kempson, on his right. The third Headmaster and First Director of Studies J W Stork is not in this picture, but the second Director of Studies, G W E Ghey is, second from the right of the same row as the Captain. Second Officer Morris, the Captain's Secretary, was the first woman on Dartmouth's staff. *(Photo College Archive).*

Some changes had to be made, because of the restrictions imposed by the blackout, and by the build-up of numbers in the College. The mistake of the First World War was not repeated, in that the size of the Dartmouth Entry was not vastly expanded with the resultant redundancies at the end of the war. However the arrival of all the special entry cadets with the withdrawal of both training cruisers meant an immediate increase in numbers of around 220. As neither the chapel nor the messroom would hold the numbers, a staggered routine became necessary. The Frobisher cadets, as they became known lived originally in the seamen's barracks, now called Beatty, but soon they also occupied 'C' block. With the appointment of the Captain as Naval Officer in Charge of Dartmouth and an area which appears to have extended from Salcombe to Beer, the Ship's company began to grow and the barracks had to be given up by the Frobishers while increasing amounts of 'A' and 'B' blocks were given over to administrative offices. Also, cadets from foreign and Commonwealth navies began to be trained in the College, cadets coming from Poland, Norway, Canada, New Zealand, South Africa, and France.

All this came suddenly to an end in September 18, 1942 when two bombs fell on the College, the first near Mr Garth's barber shop, roughly at the junction of 'O' and 'B' blocks and the second near the north-west corner of the Quarterdeck. The Q.D. and most of the classrooms were rendered unusable and all the glass was blown out of the windows of 'D' block. The College had not yet returned from summer leave and the only casualties were one Wren killed and one officer very slightly wounded. At the time of the bombing a committee was sitting in the Commander's cabin, within a very few feet of the point where the first bomb landed, discussing arrangements for evacuation should the College be bombed. *(Photo John Barlee)*.

The picture opposite shows part of the front of the College taken from the bridge. The bay window section of one of the original gunrooms, which is now in use as the engineering lecture room, has been destroyed. The picture above shows the damage from inside the Quarterdeck looking out through the hole and that below shows the damage to the roof of the Quarterdeck after some clearing work had been done. *(Photos John Barlee)*.

The College was largely uninhabitable after the bombing and permanent repairs would have to wait until happier times. The decision was taken to move the junior seven terms of the Naval College Entry to Muller's Orphanage at Ashley Down, Bristol, while the Frobishers and the Senior terms remained at Dartmouth for the time being. *(Photo John Barlee).*

The College eventually found a temporary united home in Cheshire. The Royal Naval College, Eaton Hall, certainly had a formidable aspect, as the picture opposite, bottom left, shows. Divisions had returned to a garden, a reversion to a much earlier Dartmouth, even if the presence of Wrens, opposite, top, extreme left, is a portent of things to come. Among those watching, opposite bottom right, this parade is Second Officer A M C Bulla, who was to run the catering at Eaton Hall and Dartmouth with resolute efficiency and to become a legend to generations of naval officers. *(John Barlee).*

The College might be emptied of its normal inhabitants, but Dartmouth was too useful to be left empty. Two authorities bid for the place. The Combined Operations Headquarters under Mountbatten were eventually allowed to have the College as their landing craft boat handling school despite the competing claims of the Rear Admiral Coastal Forces, who wanted a gunnery range. The picture above shows divisions during 1943 at HMS *Effingham*, with *Britannia* in her wartime drab colour scheme in yet another position. *(Photo College Archive).*

At the end of 1943 the Combined Operations establishment gave way to American units preparing for the Normandy landings. Here USN personnel are seen in the chapel. There is a window in the chapel commemorating their presence. *(Photo Western Morning News).*

CHAPTER 4

Post War Revolution

On Thursday September 19th 1946, the re-opened Royal Naval College Dartmouth accepted its first cadets, forty-two new entries who were, as usual, allocated to Drake house for their first two terms. Here we see the attentive thirteen year-olds in their gunroom in 'C' block being addressed by their house officer Lieutenant Commander R H Hodgkinson DSC.

In content the new College was generally like the one that had left in 1942. There were 550 cadets, the eleven 'Dart' Royal Naval College terms, supplemented by only one term of 'Benbow' special entry, as a training cruiser was again available. The staff comprised 30 officers and 41 masters. Yet scenes such as the one below would soon be a thing of the past. Entry at 13 had less than four years left to run, and a constant process of transformation was to begin that has continued until today. *(Radio Times Hulton Picture Library).*

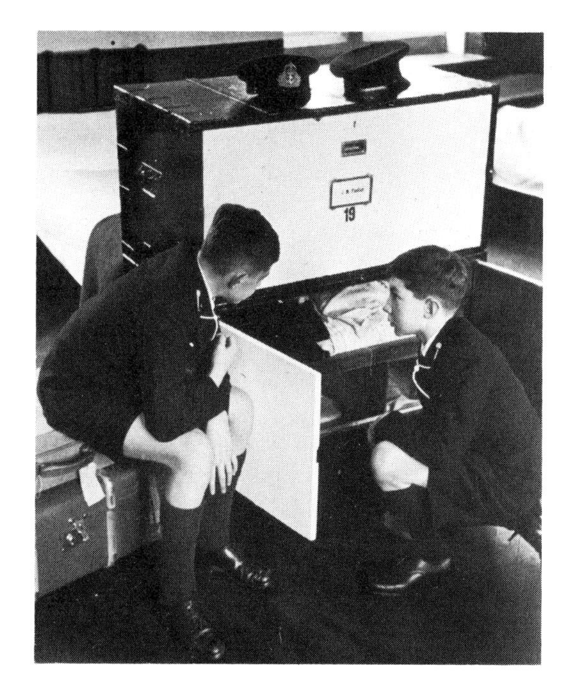

Up in the dormitories or 'chest-flats' the young cadets had to get used to stowing all their kit in their traditional sea chests. As can clearly be seen this one belongs to Cadet Jonathan M Findlay, now Commander J M Findlay RN. *(Radio Times Hulton Picture Library)*

On September 20th back came the rest of the terms and a group of senior cadets is here seen getting off the train at Kingswear. Among them was an eighth-termer, Cadet Nicholas Hunt, who was to be Captain of the College in its 75th Anniversary Year. *(Radio Times Hulton Picture Library)*.

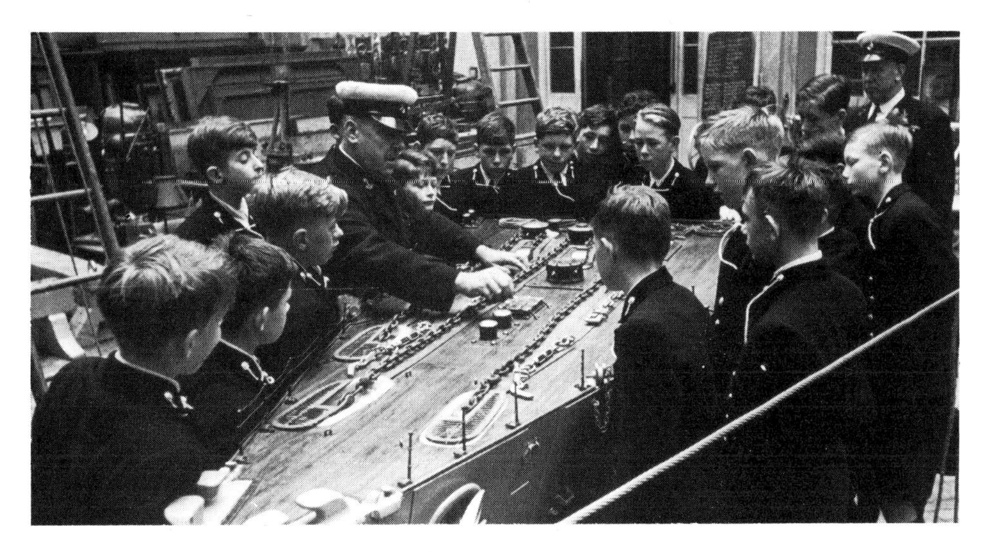

When the cadets joined, the repairs and renovation work were not quite complete and the College was in some chaos. In the seamanship room, although Mr Marks was giving instruction to the first-termers on the same old model, the equipment, much of it as familiar as the forecastle, had yet to be put back into its proper place. *(Radio Times Hulton Picture Library).*

One part of the College which was ready was the library, now expanded to take in two floors. Here in a rather 'posed' picture some young cadets are avidly using it. The effects of war and post-war 'austerity' are all too clear in the age and condition of the books. The cadets are still in shorts as a result of clothes rationing which continued at this time. *(Radio Times Hulton Picture Library).*

Classes were soon in progress and here we see a biology lesson in what is now Study 04. The teacher is the Headmaster himself, Mr J W Stork, who was to be the College's first Director of Studies. The state of the room bears witness to the recent re-occupation. None of the laboratories was, in fact, ready for use when term began. *(Radio Times Hulton Picture Library)*.

The return to Dartmouth allowed larger sailing craft to be used for training and recreation and a set of five fifty-square-metre yachts and a 65-square-metre vessel were available for the purpose as reparations from Germany. Known as 'Windfalls' they were sailed over from Cuxhaven and Kiel in August 1946 and were regular sights in the Dart until the acquisition of a new racing yacht in 1957 and five new sail training craft two years later. Here is the old *Martlet* in May 1960 at the time of her replacement by a new namesake which had been shown at the National Boat Show of that year. The 'fifty-square-metre' yacht was sold to Rear Admiral F H E Hopkins, the retiring College captain. *(College Archive)*.

The infamous winter of 1947 even affected the normally mild Dartmouth climate and there was considerable dislocation of College activities. The depth of snow coverage can easily be seen in this view of the front of the College taken from the wardroom on 30th January. *(Courtesy J F Scott)*.

A major event of the winter term of 1949 was the unveiling and dedication of the new war memorial which had been created out of the chaplain's cabin on the south side of the College just outside the chapel. The unveiling was performed by Admiral of the Fleet Lord Cunningham of Hyndhope and the dedication was conducted by the Bishop of Salisbury who had been assistant chaplain at the College in the 1920s. The main feature is a green bronze representation of a crusader ship of the type that set sail from Dartmouth for Palestine at the end of the twelfth century. The memorial was only three years old when this picture was taken. *('Illustrated')* .

Princess Margaret visited the Royal Naval College at the beginning of April 1951 to present the prizes and attend the passing-out ceremonies at the end of the spring term. On the second day of her visit she called in at HMS *Hawke*, the training establishment for 'Upper Yardmen', lower-deck officer candidates. This had just been set up in the barracks which had been vacated by the special entries in 1950. *Hawke* was run as a separate establishment and the Princess is being presented to the staff by its commanding officer, Commander G O Roberts. *Hawke* left Dartmouth in 1955 for HMS *Temeraire* in Scotland but the upper yardmen returned five years later as *Temeraire Division*. When this happened the amended ratings' uniform seen on the right of the picture was abandoned and replaced by a form of cadets' dress. The upper yardmen were integrated with the other divisions in 1962 and disappeared as a separate category in the College List in 1970. *(Courtesy D Holwill)*.

By 1952 the entry of boys at 13 had ceased, although many of the cadets in attendance had arrived at that age. Entry was now sixteen but Dartmouth was still a school and the routine was unchanged from earlier times. In the top picture opposite we see evening rounds in a chest-flat shortly after 2230. The chests are open for inspection with all their contents in correct order. The cadets are lying to attention in their beds, no doubt a little anxious as to whether anything amiss will be noticed by the inspecting officers. Woe betide any cadet who was found out! Note the alternate arrangement of the beds continues. *('Illustrated')*.

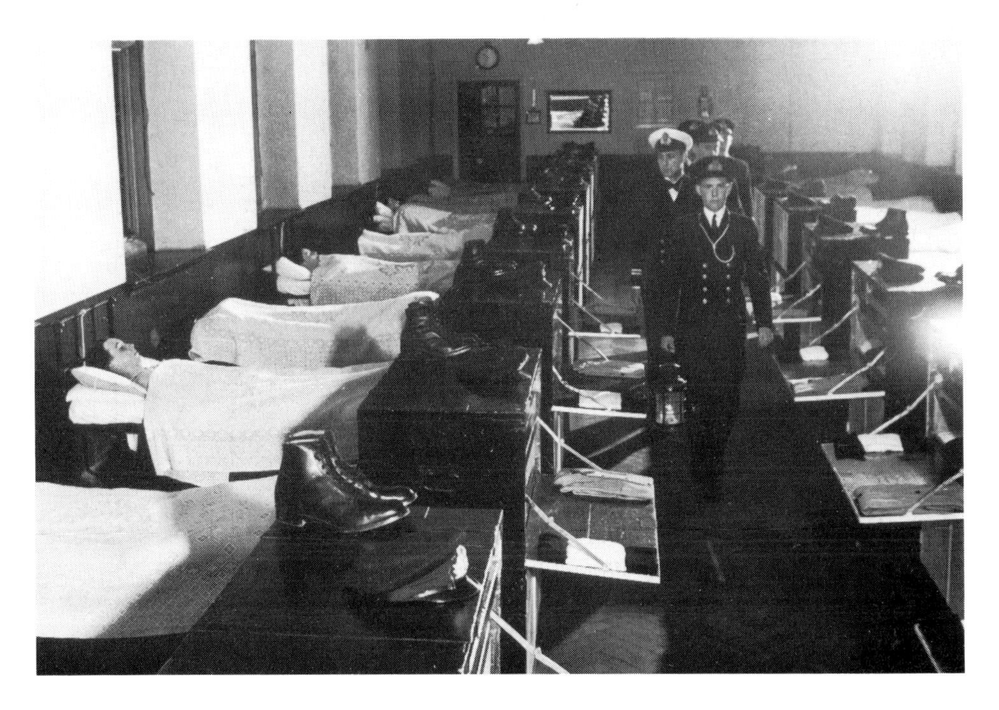

The gunrooms were still austere in 1952. This particular house seems to have done rather well in sport and yachting. *('Illustrated')*.

Music was a long established subject at the Royal Naval College and by 1952 the senior music master was Gerald E King seen here rehearsing the Chapel Choir. Mr King had arrived at Eaton Hall as a temporary assistant master at the beginning of 1943, left for a year in 1945, but came back when the College returned to Dartmouth. He retired as Director of Music in 1973 after having confirmed and extended a fine musical tradition. A multitude of naval officers owed their interest in music to Mr King's stimulation and teaching at Dartmouth. *('Illustrated')*.

Another old established tradition still going on in 1952 was dancing on the quarterdeck in order to learn that vital social attribute of the naval officer's ambassadorial role. *('Illustrated')*.

Eighteen-year-old 'special' or 'public school' entry cadets had been at Dartmouth since 1939. At first they had been housed in the barracks but by 1952 they were living in the main College buildings and being instructed in 'E' and 'F' blocks, the second of which is seen here. This new building had only been complete for a short time but was soon to close temporarily as numbers in the College declined in the early 'fifties. The special entry's one-term course was of purely professional instruction and these two cadets are working at navigation under the supervision of Instructor Lt Cdr Finch. After a term at Dartmouth they passed on to a training cruiser, by then HMS *Devonshire.* The separate 'special entry' was abolished on the introduction of a complete 'eighteen entry' in 1955. 'F' block was then re-opened for navigational and communications training. *('Illustrated').*

For the Coronation in 1953, 100 Dartmouth cadets were given the task of lining the route of the procession in Parliament Square. Here they are seen being given instruction in the task on the College parade ground. Other cadets were part of the naval contingent in the procession itself. All cadets also went to the Coronation Review at Spithead being accommodated in the training carriers *Implacable* and *Indefatigable. (The Rt Reverend G K Giggal OBE, RN).*

In July 1954 Prince Philip came to Dartmouth in HM Yacht *Britannia* to unveil a plaque in town commemorating the Allied landings in France and to pay a private visit to the College. This was the first time *Britannia* had been in the Dart since her commissioning in January which had forced the College to change its name the previous year to 'Britannia Royal Naval College, HMS Dartmouth'. While at the College, the Prince, who had been one of the first term of special entries to come to Dartmouth in 1939, was shown the experimental cabin in 'C' block. This was the first sign of the metamorphosis that was to change Dartmouth from a school into a fully-fledged naval academy. On the right of the picture can be seen the *Mew* the famous and long lived railway ferry. *(J Barlee)*.

The College's golden jubilee was celebrated at the beginning of July 1955. On Saturday the 2nd there was a garden party and the last of the traditional cricket matches between Admirals and Cadets. In the evening a Jubilee Dinner was held at which there were five former Captains of the College and numerous old Dartmouth staff and pupils. At 2230 the grand finale was a firework display seen here helping light up that memorable summer's evening. *(College Archive)*.

The new eighteen entry COST scheme of 1955 necessitated many alterations to the College's interior layout. The old large 'chest-flats' became cabins like this four-berth example in Blake Division photographed in 1977. In these and the new single cabins the cadets and midshipmen could study in private as well as sleep. The bedspreads have not changed! *(C Risk)*.

The older entry required more relaxed and adult messing facilities. The old house gunrooms were refurbished and the senior gunroom in 'A' block was converted into an ante-room bar for the officers-under-training. It is seen in 1963 shortly before further alterations were made to improve facilities for the sub lieutenants of the 1960s. *(College Archive)*.

A vital part of the COST Scheme was the creation of a Dartmouth Training Squadron to give cadets and midshipmen sea experience during their training. For the longer voyages, especially in the three months 'Phase II' training, a 'First Division' of three ships was provided. These were usually 2100 ton 'Type 15 Conversion' ASW frigates but the destroyer HMS *Carron* was also used. Here we see, in the Dart, the Type 15 HMS *Venus*, one of the original ships of 1956. Clearly visible are the extra open bridge built on top of the closed original and the deck house for instructional space abaft it. *Venus* served in the DTS until 1961 when she helped take the first 'Murray Scheme' cadets to sea. The other frigates deployed in the Squadron in the period 1956–61 were HMS *Vigilant, Roebuck, Urchin, Ulysses* and *Wizard*. During this time the squadron was used operationally both in exercises and for fishery protection off Iceland. *(College Archive).*

For shorter-distance work and day-running two 1040 ton 'Algerine' class minesweepers, HMS *Jewel* and HMS *Acute* formed the 'Second Division' of DTS in 1956. Here is the second of the pair and the extra accommodation to fit her for her role as a training ship can be seen aft. After seventeen terms and over a thousand midshipmen being schooled in the various arts of navigation, seaboat drill, buoywork, jackstay and minesweeping the two ships left the Dart in 1961 with the end of the COST Scheme. *(College Archive).*

The coming of a Royal Marine Band at the beginning of 1956 marked the end of the Voluntary College Band which had played for parades and other functions since the start of the establishment's history. Here is the final group of cadets and civilian staff photographed in late 1955. In the background is the figurehead in its first post-war colour scheme. *(Courtesy D Holwill).*

To mark the fiftieth anniversary of the College and the happy relations with Dartmouth town over the years the Council decided to present BRNC with the Freedom of the Borough. The ceremonial presentation by the Mayor, Mrs Dorothy Holwill, took place on the New Ground, Dartmouth on a cold and snowy Wednesday February 22nd 1956. After the presentation parade the cadets marched round the town to pass a saluting base at the Quay. Mrs Holwill can be seen taking the salute with, behind her, the College Captain, W G Crawford. Also present at the ceremony were the First Lord of the Admiralty, Viscount Cilcennin and the Fourth Sea Lord, Rear Admiral A D Watson. *(Courtesy D Holwill).*

During the Summer Term of 1958 great preparations were made for a Royal Visit at the end of term passing-out parade during which a Queen's Colour would be presented to the College. *(Courtesy Captain J C K Slater).*

During the COST scheme air familiarisation was carried out in 'Phase II' period by 727 Squadron at RNAS Brawdy. From 1960, however, two Dragonfly 5 helicopters were based at Dartmouth as 'Britannia Helicopter Flight'. Maintenance was at first carried out at Manadon but these facilities were later provided at the operating base at Norton that was built in a corner of the College's additional playing fields. The original aim was to provide helicopter experience for all cadets and to give elementary helicopter direction exercises with the DTS. The formation of the flight reflected the planned adoption of the helicopter as an integral part of the equipment of the modern fleet but it became even more important given the beginning of supplementary-list aircrew training at the College. A full air department was formed in 1960 at BRNC with Tiger Moths, later Chipmunks, at Roborough. In the mid 1960s the Dragonflies were replaced by a more modern Wasp. *(College Archive).*

The stimulus of 'Unison 63', a study gathering of senior representatives of the Commonwealth armed forces, planned by Lord Mountbatten, Chief of the Defence Staff, caused the building of a much needed large hall. The hall's architects were Messrs Playne Lacey and Partners, Westminster which now incorporated Sir Aston Webb & Son. The hall/theatre was intended to seat 485 and was for general purposes from musical recitals (previously held in the chapel or gymnasium) to examinations. It was first used by Admiral of the Fleet Sir Caspar John to address the passers-out in the summer of 1963 and was duly christened 'Caspar John Hall'. 'Unison' took place in September and twelve nations were represented by the 220 guests. *(College Archive)*.

The introduction of the eighteen entry caused the re-conversion of 'D' block mess-room to its original role of 'Junior Gunroom'. The austere working rig adopted for the 'Murray Scheme' first-termers is clearly seen in the 1965 view, the original recommendation for ratings' uniforms not having been adopted. The more senior cadets are in normal cadets' uniform. *(College Archive)*.

By 1963 the seamanship room had become the air lecture room suitably decorated with models such as a Fairey Gannet ASW aircraft, and various pictures of naval aviation past and present. Especially notable is the photograph of Squadron Commander Dunning's first landing on *Furious* in 1917. The decision to abandon fixed-wing carriers is symbolised by this 1966 view of the same room converted into a 'Fleet Display Room' to illustrate the organisation, strength and deployment of the entire contemporary Royal Navy. In the era when 'East of Suez' loomed large the map was able to show the world wide distribution of HM Ships such as the four-year-old guided missile destroyer *Devonshire* displayed in model form in front of it. All the display has now disappeared, as out-of-date in the 1980s as the model of the World War One battle-cruiser was in the '60s. *(College Archive).*

Work began at the end of 1968 on building a new main road, 'College Way', into Dartmouth down the south-western portion of the 'Britannia Estate'. The old layout is clearly seen in this 1968 view which also shows in the left foreground the Rock Park married quarters built in the late 1950s. The hospital block, by now Hawke Division and naval stores, can be clearly seen with its three ex-isolation wards and to its left are the pavilion and playing fields. Moving past the new senior officers' houses and 1906 lecturers' hostel we come to the College itself with Caspar John Hall clearly visible to its left. The landscaped grounds, a tribute to their designer Mr Milner, had been converted into a nine hole golf course the previous year. *(C Risk).*

A custom which disappeared in 1971 was the pay parade on the quarterdeck and the last of these occasions is illustrated overleaf. By this time the cadets were receiving real pay although the original participants in such occasions only got pocket money provided by their parents. Cadet captains did, however, get pay from the Admiralty for their additional duties. The officers giving out the money are the contemporary seniors, third-year sub lieutenants. The blend of new conditions in an old context is typical of the Dartmouth tradition of continuity. The US Navy officer, in the picture overleaf top, is BRNC's second USN liaison officer, Lt Cdr James J Hogan. The Dartmouth 'cadet' had only a few more months of life for in 1972 all the juniors were to become midshipmen as part of the new Naval College Entry scheme. *(C Risk).*

The first direct graduate entries arrived at Dartmouth in 1964 and by 1971 were an accepted part of the Dartmouth scene. A rather more notable member of the 'accelerated stream' of September was Sub Lieutenant The Prince of Wales who passed out at half term. Dartmouth now provides the professional training to all the Royal Navy's graduate entries as well as giving some academic instruction in technical subjects to arts graduates. *(C Risk).*

By the time the Queen visited the College in 1972 the new order of midshipmen was much in evidence. The summer passing-out parade had become Lord High Admiral's Divisions two years before but this was the first time that Her Majesty had attended in person as Lord High Admiral. With the new Naval College Entry scheme of training, the timing of this parade, the most important of the term, was altered to the end of the Easter term from 1975. *(C Risk).*

The end of the Murray Scheme also marked the end of the Dartmouth Training Squadron which paid a farewell visit to the College in the summer term of 1972. 'Type 12' ASW frigates had begun to replace the converted Type 15s in 1963 and from then until 1972 the squadron had been made up of various combinations of HMS *Torquay*, *Scarborough*, *Tenby* and *Eastbourne*. The last three of these formed the final squadron and here is HMS *Scarborough*, the final leader, sailing down the Dart for the last time trailing her paying-off pennant. She and the other two frigates were escorted by the College's picket boats. On the left is one of the ex-battleship boats which had been used since the College's return. On the right is one of the first 'GRPs' which have since replaced all the older craft. *(C Risk).*

The new Dartmouth Training Ship was the assault ship HMS *Intrepid* which with only one short break, has shared the task with her sister HMS *Fearless* since 1972. Here, *Fearless* is seen (left) in January 1975 on her first commission as DTS, alongside her French counterpart the helicopter carrier/training ship *Jeanne D'Arc*. They met in Caribbean waters on a cruise that took the embarked midshipmen and direct-graduate-entry sub lieutenants to St Lucia, Barbados, St Vincent, Venezuela, the Virgin Islands, Cartagena and Bermuda. The new 'ship' is no less an operational unit than the previous 'squadron' and as well as regularly taking part in exercises with Marines embarked, is fully capable of being deployed to a trouble spot if required. *(HMS Fearless)*.

The first female officers under training at BRNC were the eight QARNNS sisters who formed the first Short Introductory Course of Spring 1973. They are here seen posed on the ramps with a group of first term 'International' midshipmen marching by during a parade-training period. Both the advent of ladies and the large numbers of foreign OUTs were important features of BRNC in the 1970s. *(C Risk)*.

1974 saw the arrival of the officer candidates for the Special Duties list who had formerly been trained in HMS *St George* at Eastney. The SD Candidates, Petty Officers and Chief Petty Officers form a separate 'St George Division' for their one-term course. Here is the passing-out class of Christmas 1977. *(C Risk).*

We have followed the story of the seamanship room through many changes and this shows it as it was in 1977. The old battleship forecastle that arrived in 1931 is still in residence but the setting has now changed to one of the old gun-rooms in 'B' block next to the chapel. *(C Risk).*

In September 1976 WRNS Officer training was transferred to Dartmouth from RNC Greenwich. The course forms 'Talbot' Division along the same lines as St George, although the one-term academic and professional course is very different! Here are members of the first group of Talbot girls returning from a cruise in HMS *Walkerton*, the College's tender at this time. A small minesweeper had been attached to the College since 1961 first to give sea experience to SL aircrew but latterly to give general navigational and seamanship 'back-up' to the shore training. HMS *Brearley* was replaced by HMS *Repton* at the end of 1968 and she in turn was replaced by *Walkerton* in 1970. After becoming a feature of River Dart life *Walkerton* was replaced by the patrol vessels *Sandpiper* and *Peterel* in 1979. *(C Risk).*

Given the College's royal connections it is perhaps only fitting that, in its 75th anniversary year, BRNC should contain a royal officer-under-training, Midshipman The Prince Andrew, an SL airman of '93 Flight' (official consecutive numbering of such entries began with '17 Entry' in 1965). Here the Prince is seen on arrival in September 1979 with Captain Hunt who took over command at the end of 1978, thirty-two years after entering as a cadet from Eaton Hall.